Dying To Self: A Golden Dialogue

William Law

The Spirit of Love

DYING TO SELF

A GOLDEN DIALOGUE

BY

WILLIAM LAW

WITH NOTES BY

REV. ANDREW MURRAY

London

JAMES NISBET & CO., LIMITED

21 BERNERS STREET

1898

DYING TO SELF

Printed by BALLANTYNE, HANSON & CO.
At the Ballantyne Press

PREFACE

In the introductory lecture to his "Character and Characteristics of William Law," Dr. Whyte writes, "I wish some student of Law had reprinted for the Christian public the third and practical part of the 'Spirit of Love.'" Elsewhere he speaks of it as A Golden Dialogue. In this issue of the Dialogue I have left out what appeared to have no direct reference to the practical part of the "Spirit of Love." In the notes I have tried to help some readers, who might not at once be able to take in Law's teaching, and might not be ready to give the careful and continued study needed to master his thoughtful style, to see what really the points are that he wishes to open up and enforce.

His chief thoughts are these. The ordinary Christian life is a state of pupilage, in which, under the influence of the teaching of Scripture, mind and heart have to be educated and disciplined, and the will trained and stirred, to seek after a life in which the

Spirit of Love really fills and rules the soul. Such a life is possible, but can be received only by the operation of God, in which our Lord, as the Lamb of God, reveals Himself in the heart and takes possession. The great, in fact the one real hindrance to this life of the Spirit of Love within us, is the power of our evil self, that poisons our whole nature. The chief object of our time of pupilage, and that on which its length and its issue depend, is that the soul, in its struggle to obey God's law and to overcome this evil self with its tempers, be brought to the confession of its own utter impotence to work deliverance. The only way to deliverance is by a true and entire death to self. The great secret of this death to self—this is really the secret of his teaching and the central thought of the Dialogue—the great secret of the death to self, is to be found in a simple helpless turning from self to God. This dying to self is the very perfection of faith in Christ as the Lamb of God. At first sight it does not appear how this can bring such a wonderful deliverance from self, or lead to Christ's rising on the soul with the light of heaven, and the full birth of the Spirit of Love. But as he expounds the truth, and shows how in the humility of the Lamb of God lay the secret of the work He did, and the salvation He gives, and how the sinking down before God in humility, meekness, patience, and resignation to God is the very perfection of faith in Christ, and the one only condition of God's doing His work in us, we are compelled to acknowledge that here is indeed the place of blessing.

A great deal has been said against the use of terms like The Higher Life, and A Second Blessing. In Law one finds nothing of such language, but of the deep truth of which they are the, perhaps defective, expression his whole book is full. The points on which so much stress is laid in what is called Keswick Teaching, stand prominently out in his whole argument. The low state of the average life of the believer, the cause of all failure as coming from self-confidence, the need of an entire surrender of the whole being to the operation of God, the call to turn to Christ in faith as the one and sure Deliverer from the power of self, the Divine certainty of a better life for all who will in self-despair trust Christ for it, and the heavenly joy of a life in which the Spirit of Love fills the heart—these truths are common property. What appears to make Law's putting of the truth of special value, is the way in which he shows how humility and utter self-despair, with the resignation to God's mighty working in simple faith, is the infallible way to be delivered from self and have the Spirit of Love fill the heart.

I pray that the blessing and help his teaching has been to myself may be shared by many, and that this little book may be used of God to open up the exceeding riches of His Grace in Christ Jesus.

ANDREW MURRAY.

WELLINGTON,
   July 11, 1898.

Some may object to the title "Dying to Self." I have tried in Note A to explain my view of it as connected with our being dead to sin in Christ.

INTRODUCTION

BEFORE commencing our study of this Dialogue, it may be well to point out the place it has in the work of which it is a part.

Law's book on the Spirit of Love consists of two parts. In the First Part he gives a summary, which he works out more fully in the second. He begins with God as the origin of all love, because He is *an eternal and immutable will to all goodness.* Let the reader hold fast this definition of the nature of God. It is one of Law's axioms from which he makes two important deductions : that in virtue of His very nature, God delights to give all goodness, happiness, and blessing, and can give nothing else ; and that there can be no possible good in any creature but what God gives. All that Scripture teaches us of dependence upon God and faith in Him depends upon these two primary truths.

Because this love in God is the original of all love in the creature, love can be nothing in us but what it is in God, *a will to all goodness toward others, at all times and on all occasions.* And this Spirit of Love is not really yours till it is the spirit of your life, till you live freely, willingly, universally according to it. The Spirit of Love can do nothing but love, wherever it is, and whatever is done to it,

ix

because it is the truth and reality of God in the soul.

Thus love is the one only bond of union between God and the creature. As the will to all goodness is the whole nature of God, so it must be the whole nature of every service or religion that can be acceptable to Him.

All sin is nothing but the spirit of the creature turned from the universality of love to some self-seeking or own will in created things.

It is this self that crucified Christ, the Lord God. It is from this self sinful man must be purified. And there is no way of being thus purified, but by dying to self and having the Spirit of Love born in us. This is the absolute necessity of the Gospel doctrine of the cross, viz., of dying to self as the one only way to life in God.

In the Second Part there are three Dialogues. In the FIRST the twofold life of the creature is laid open, as it either exists for that for which it was created, to receive and manifest the goodness of God, or as it is in itself, without God. And so, because goodness and happiness are absolutely inseparable from God, and can be nowhere but in God, *the life of God in union with the creaturely life* is the one only possibility of goodness and happiness in any creature, whether in heaven or earth.

To this end a perpetual, always acting operation of the Spirit of God within us is absolutely necessary. The holiness of the Christian is not an occasional thing, that begins or ends, or is only for a certain time, or place, or action, but is the holiness of that which is *always alive and stirring in us*, namely, of our thoughts, wills, desires, and affections. If our thoughts and affections are to be always holy and good, then the Holy and Good Spirit of God is to be *always operating* as a principle of life within us.

The kingdom of heaven must be all within us, or it never can possibly belong to us. Goodness, piety, holiness can only be ours as *thinking, willing, and desiring are ours, by being in us as a power of heaven in the birth and growth of our own life.*

And now, since the one only work of Christ as your Redeemer is only this, to take from the earthly life of flesh and blood its usurped power, all you have to do or can do is to resist, and, as far as you can, renounce the evil tempers and workings of your own evil nature. You want no other deliverance but from *the power of your earthly self.* Nothing that we do is bad, but because it *resists the working and power of God within us;* and nothing that we do can be good, but because it *conforms to the Spirit of God within us.* And thus you see your salvation consists *wholly and solely in the life of God,* or Christ as God, quickened and born again in you; in other words, in the restoration and perfect union of the first twofold life in humanity.

In the SECOND Dialogue Law explains the way of salvation through Jesus Christ. He points out how, as the second Adam, He could be the parent of a new humanity. He had to enter into our state, and, in its weakness and sufferings, pass through that which we needed to pass through in giving up and departing

from the life of fallen nature. He could not show
that He was not of this world, that He lived in the
perfection of the first man, but by showing that *all the
good of this earthly life was renounced by Him*, and
that *all the evil which the world*, the malice of men or
devils, *could bring upon Him, could not hinder His
living wholly and solely* to God, and doing His will
with the same fulness as it is done in heaven.
Wonder not, then, that the true followers of Christ,
the saints of every age, have so gloried in the
cross of Christ, have desired nothing so much as
to be partakers of it, to live in constant union
with it.

It is this whole process of Jesus Christ, through
which He passed, and through which He leads us,
that is the only possible means that heaven or earth
can afford to save man from himself. And thus the
sufferings and death of Christ are not only consistent
with the doctrine of a God all love, but are the fullest
and most absolute proof of it.

At the close of this argument Eusebius answers, "I
am now in full possession of this most glorious truth,
that God is mere love, the most glorious truth that
can possess and edify the heart of man. I want to
return home, and enjoy my Bible, and delight myself
with reading it in the comfortable light in which you
have set the whole ground and nature of our redemption. Therefore, dear Theophilus, adieu! God is
love, and he that hath learnt to live in the Spirit of
Love hath learnt to live and dwell in God.

"*Theophilus.*—God prosper the spark of heaven in
your soul. But, before you leave me, I beg one more

conversation, to be on the practical part of the Spirit of Love; that so doctrine and practice, hearing and doing, may go hand in hand."

THE THIRD DIALOGUE.

It may help us to see whither Law wants to lead us in this Dialogue, treating of the practical application of his teaching, and what the way is in which he proposes to reach the goal, if we take a survey of his line of argument. The Dialogue may be divided into four sections. In the first, he points out to his friends the immense difference between intellectual and spiritual apprehension, between the delightful impression that can be made by an insight into a truth, and its actual possession. Any one in a hurry to come to Law's teaching about Dying to Self might pass over this portion, and think that he missed nothing of the real argument. That would be perfectly true. And yet he might miss what is of far more importance than the argument—the right spirit in which to approach, and in which alone to profit by it, so as to obtain an entrance into the blessed life he speaks of. Because the Dying to Self and the Living to God is the exchange of one life for another, the losing the one to gain the other, he makes plain in the second section how the difference between Light and Darkness is the image of the intense, irreconcilable, and eternal difference between the life of God and the life of Self. It is only when this is fully believed that there can be even the beginning of the capacity to understand what Dying to Self is. After having thus prepared his reader, the third section unfolds the simple but wonderful secret of Dying to Self as the one infallible way to what constitutes true salvation—the life of God restored in man.

The fourth section treats of the actual enjoyment of this blessing.

CONTENTS

THIRD SECTION.—OF DYING TO SELF TO LIVE TO GOD

FOURTH SECTION.—OF THE LIFE OF GOD IN THE SOUL

THE SPIRIT OF LOVE

SECOND PART

THE THIRD DIALOGUE

FIRST SECTION

OF INTELLECTUAL AND SPIRITUAL APPREHENSION

1. *The Difference between Admiring and Possessing*

Eusebius.—You have shown great good-will towards us, Theophilus, in desiring another meeting before we leave you. But yet I seem to myself to have no need of that which you have proposed by this day's conversation. For this doctrine of the Spirit of Love cannot have more power over me, or be more deeply rooted in me, than it is already. It has so gained and got possession of my whole heart that everything else must be under its dominion. I can do nothing else but love; it is my whole nature; I have no taste for anything else. Can this matter be carried higher in practice?

Theophilus.—No higher, Eusebius. And was this the true state of your heart, you would bid fair to leave

A

the world as Elijah did ; or, like Enoch, to have it
said of you, that you lived wholly to love, and was not.
For was there nothing but this Divine love alive in
you, your fallen flesh and blood would be in danger
of being quite burnt up by it. What you have said
of yourself, you have spoken in great sincerity, but
in a total ignorance of yourself, and the true nature
of the Spirit of Divine Love. You are as yet only
charmed with the sight, or rather the sound, of it ;
its real birth is as yet unfelt and unfound in you.
Your natural complexion has a great deal of the
animal meekness and softness of the lamb and the
dove, your blood and spirit are of this turn ; and
therefore a God all love, and a religion all love,
quite transport you ; and you are so delighted with
it, that you fancy you have nothing in you but this
God and religion of love. But, my friend, bear with
me, if I tell you that all this is only the good part
of the spirit of this bestial world in you, and may be
in any unregenerate man that is of your complexion.
It is so far from being a genuine fruit of Divine love,
that, if it be not well looked to, it may prove a real
hindrance of it, as it oftentimes does, by its appear-
ing to be that which it is not.

You have quite forgot all that was said in the letter
to you on the Spirit of Love, that it is a birth in the
soul, that can only come forth in its proper time and
place, and from its proper causes. Now nothing that
is a birth can be taken in or brought into the soul
by any notional conception or delightful apprehension of it. You may love it as much as you please,
think it the most charming thing in the world,

fancy everything but dross and dung in comparison
of it, and yet have no more of its birth in you than
the blind man has of that light of which he has
got a most charming notion. His blindness still
continues the same; he is at the same distance from
the light, because light can only be had by a birth
of itself in seeing eyes. It is thus with the Spirit
of Love; it is nowhere but where it rises up as
a birth.

The great message Law has in this book is, that the
Spirit of Love can only come into us as a Divine birth,
by which it becomes our very life, making love natural
to us. The great hindrance in the way of those who
are in earnest in seeking it is that they get deceived,
and delight themselves with what is not the actual
possession of that which they admire. A beautiful
picture of a landscape on our wall may be a daily
feast, while we never think of possessing the property.
Even so, beautiful views and impressions of heavenly
things, and specially of a life in the Spirit of Love, may
occupy and gratify us, while in practice we are very far
from possessing them.

Law's deep spiritual insight had taught him that here
was to be found, in a multitude of cases, the cause of
failure in the spiritual life. Every minister who asks
earnestly why the preaching of the Word to believers
does not work more effectually to produce humble, holy,
heavenly living, has found one of his chief answers
here. Men are delighted, and, as they think, greatly
edified by the clear and striking setting forth of spiritual
truth, while they never know that it demands the surrender of the whole life and will, the actual death to

the world and to self, if these truths are really to become their personal possession. They need to be taught, and it is no easy lesson to teach or to learn, that the mind can do nothing but form pictures and images of Divine things; it is only by God's direct operation, waited on and allowed to work in us, that the original of the picture, the substance and reality of which the image was a shadow, can become an actual possession.

Study Law's portrait and treatment of Eusebius. He was so filled with admiration and delight of what he had heard of love in God and in us, that he did not think it could have more power than it had already; he was sure it had permeated his whole heart. Theophilus shows him his mistake; because he was delighted with the thoughts, he fancied that he was filled with God and His love. He was still entirely ignorant of what was meant by, and needed for, the birth of love within the soul.

This is the lesson this Golden Dialogue offers to teach us. It offers to lead us to the place where the Spirit of Love can be our life, and can have its abiding rule in us. As it sets open the gate, it gives us the one solemn warning: Beware of thinking that when you understand and approve of and enjoy the teaching, when it brings you light and pleasure, and calls forth new sentiments and energies—beware of thinking you possess it. All this lies in the region of thought and feeling. It is only by a Divine birth ruling your very being and nature that you really can possess it.

Soul

Spirit

2. *The Spirit of Love and the Price to be Paid for its Possession.*

Eusebius.—But if I am got no farther than this, what good have I from giving in so heartily to all that you have said of this doctrine? And to what end have you taken so much pains to assert and establish it?

Theophilus.—Your error lies in this; you confound two things which are entirely distinct from each other. You make no difference betwixt the doctrine that only sets forth the nature, excellency, and necessity of the Spirit of Love, and the Spirit of Love itself; which yet are two things so different, that you may be quite full of the former, and at the same time quite empty of the latter. I have said everything that I could to show you the truth, excellency, and necessity of the Spirit of Love : it is of infinite importance to you to be well established in the belief of this doctrine. But all that I have said of it is only to induce and encourage you to buy it at its own price, and to give all that for it which alone can purchase it. But if you think (as you plainly do) that you have got it, because you are so highly pleased with that which you have heard of it, you only embrace the shadow, instead of the substance, of that which you ought to have.

Eusebius.—What is the price that I must give for it?

Theophilus.—You must give up all that you are and all that you have from fallen Adam; for all that you are and have from him is that life of flesh and blood which cannot enter into the kingdom of God.

Adam, after his fall, had nothing that was good in him, nothing that could inherit an eternal life in heaven, but the bruiser of the serpent, or the seed of the Son of God, that was inspoken into him. Everything else in him was devoted to death, that this incorruptible seed of the Word might grow up into a new name in Christ Jesus.

Eusebius.—Now, proceed as you please to lay open all my defects, in the Spirit of Love; for I am earnestly desirous of being set right in so important a matter.

Theogenes.—Let me first observe to Theophilus, that I am afraid the matter is much worse with me than it is with you. For though this doctrine seems to have got all my heart, as it is a doctrine; yet I am continually thrown out of it in practice, and find myself as daily under the power of my old tempers and passions as I was before I was so full of this doctrine.

———————

Eusebius cannot understand what Theophilus means. He has accepted the teaching so heartily, and feels so ready to live it out, that he cannot imagine what is lacking. He has never learnt that one may be full of the doctrine of love, and yet without its spirit. He does not know that all teaching about spiritual truth is only a finger-post pointing the way to something that has to be purchased at a great price, and that all the pleasure the teaching gives is only to lure us on to pay the price needed to secure the treasure.

The parable of the treasure in the field is a favourite

one with Law. He points out how the man who found the treasure rejoiced over it before it was his, and how, if he had not sold all to buy the field, it would have availed him little. The joy of discovering the treasure is the happiness which an insight into the beauty of Divine truth brings; it may be renewed every Sabbath as we listen to Gospel preaching, and every day as we study our Bible, and yet leave us as poor as we were. Never imagine that the pleasure we have in the word is a guarantee that it is being a blessing to us. This is not so; but till we pay the price, only as we daily pay the price, will the truth in its power, will the Spirit of Love really be ours.

And what is the price? "You must give up all that you are, and all that you have from fallen Adam." The Spirit of Love is a new life; nothing less than giving up all our own life is the price to be paid. We have here, at the very opening, the dying to self made the one condition of the actual enjoyment of the life of God. We are not meant ever to live the mixed life, in which the old man has the upper hand. The Spirit of Love waits to fill us as soon as we are ready to buy, without holding back part of the price.

You must give up all: all you *have* and all you *are*, from fallen Adam. That is meant literally. All we are and have from Adam is sinful: it must all be given up. Our very life, Christ said, must be hated, must be lost. Before a man consents to this, it needs Divine teaching to make him see that all our natural life is indeed so incurably evil as to need being given up and parted with. When he does see and consent to this, it needs time and Divine teaching to show him what the giving up all, this dying to self, really means. When he sees and consents to this, it needs Divine teaching to bring him to believe that, if he pay the price, the hidden treasure of a nature that can love, that always will love, is to be found.

If we want to learn these lessons and get possession, let us beware, above all else, of taking our delight in the discovery of the treasure for possession, lest we have to complain with Theogenes: "Though this doctrine seems to have got all my heart, yet I am continually thrown out of it in practice, and find myself as daily under the power of my old tempers and passions as I was before I was so full of it."

✳ 3. *Two Ways of Seeking Goodness.*

Theophilus.—You are to know, my friends, that every kind of virtue and goodness may be brought into us by two different ways. They may be **taught us outwardly** by men, by rules and precepts; and they may be **inwardly born** in us, as **the genuine birth of our own renewed spirit.** In the former way, as we learn them only from men, by rules and documents of instruction, they at best only change our outward behaviour, and leave our heart in its natural state, and only put our passions under a forced restraint, which will occasionally break forth in spite of the dead letter of precept and doctrine. Now this way of learning and attaining goodness, though thus imperfect, is yet **absolutely necessary in the nature of the thing,** and must first have its time, and place, and work in us; yet it is only for a time, as the law was a schoolmaster to the gospel. We must first be babes in doctrine, as well as in strength, before we can be men. But of all this outward in-

struction, whether from good men or the letter of
Scripture, it must be said, as the Apostle saith of the
law, that "it maketh nothing perfect;" and yet is
highly necessary in order to perfection.

The true perfection and profitableness of the holy
written Word of God is fully set forth by St. Paul to
Timothy; "From a child (saith he) thou hast known
the Scriptures, which are able to make thee wise unto
salvation, which is by faith in Christ Jesus." Now
these Scriptures were the Law and the Prophets, for
Timothy had known no other from his youth. And
as they, so all other Scriptures since, have no other
good or benefit in them, but as they lead and direct
us to a salvation that is not to be had in themselves, but from faith in Christ Jesus. Their teaching is only to teach us where to seek and to find
the fountain and source of all light and knowledge.

Of the Law, saith the Apostle, "it was a schoolmaster to Christ;" of the Prophets, he saith the
same. "Ye have (says he) a more sure word of prophecy; whereunto you do well that ye take heed, as
unto a light that shineth in a dark place, until the
day dawn, and the daystar ariseth in your hearts."
The same thing is to be affirmed of the letter of the
New Testament; it is but our schoolmaster unto
Christ, a light like that of prophecy, to which we are
to take great heed, until Christ, as the dawning of
the day, or the daystar, ariseth in our hearts. Nor
can the thing possibly be otherwise; no instruction
that comes under the form of words can do more
for us than sounds and words can do; they can only
direct us to something that is better than them-

selves, that can be the true light, life, spirit, and power of holiness in us.

Eusebius.—I cannot deny what you say, and yet it seems to me to derogate from Scripture.

Theophilus.—Would you then have me to say that the written word of God is that Word of God which liveth and abideth for ever; that Word which is the wisdom and power of God; that Word which was with God, which was God, by whom all things were made; that Word of God which was made flesh for the redemption of the world; that Word of God, of which we must be born again; that Word which "lighteth every man that cometh into the world;" that Word which in Christ Jesus "is become wisdom, and righteousness, and sanctification in us;" would you have me say that all this is to be understood of the written word of God? But if this cannot possibly be, then all that I have said is granted, namely, that Jesus is alone that Word of God that can be the light, life, and salvation of fallen man. Or how is it possible more to exalt the letter of Scripture, than by owning it to be a true, outward, verbal direction to the one only true light and salvation of man.

Suppose you had been a true disciple of John the Baptist, whose only office was to prepare the way to Christ, how could you have more magnified his office, or declared your fidelity to him, than by going from his teaching to be taught by that Christ to whom he directed you? The Baptist was, indeed, a "burning and a shining light," and so are the Holy Scriptures; but "he was not that light, but was sent to bear witness of that light. That was the true light, which lighteth every man that cometh into the world."

What a folly would it be to say that you had undervalued the office and character of John the Baptist, because he was not allowed to be the light itself, but only a true witness of it, and guide to it? Now if you can show that the written word in the Bible can have any other or higher office or power than such a ministerial one as the Baptist had, I am ready to hear you.

Theophilus had brought his friends to see the difference between intellectual and spiritual apprehension, between the joy of finding a treasure and the deeper joy of possessing it; and also, what was of more importance, to admit that they did not yet possess the Spirit of Love. He now proceeds to show them what their present state is, both as regards that which is good and desirable in it, and that which is still wanting in it.

In all education there are two ways of leading men in the path of truth and virtue. The one is by outward instruction and authority, seeking to inculcate self-control, to foster habits, and to waken desires. The other is by inspiration, when the teacher is able to breathe into his pupil the very disposition that animates himself. God deals no otherwise in the education of His people or the individual Christian. First came the law to prepare the way; then came grace and truth, the power and reality of the Divine life in Christ Jesus. In the individual believer the process is the same. The new birth brings him as a child into a state of grace in which he is shown what the stature of the perfect man in Christ is, is taught to desire and to strive after it, and is led on to expect and receive it. The deadly mistake in the life of most Christians is, that they rest content with the preparatory stage, and either do not believe in the prospect of spiritual maturity that is held out, or are not willing to pay the price needed to obtain it.

Law makes very clear how we are to regard this preparatory stage. On the one hand, it is imperfect and not to be rested in, however delightful its glimpses and foretastes of the better state; on the other, it is necessary, even indispensable to perfection. He points out how the Scriptures have their great value from this double point of view. While they teach and discipline and strengthen and influence us, they always point away from themselves to a salvation which they cannot give, but is only to be had from God Himself. Their teaching only serves to direct us to what they cannot give us, to lead us to Him who gives the true spiritual teaching. " They direct us to what is better than themselves, that can be the true life, light, spirit, and power of holiness in us."

In answer to the scruple that this appears to derogate from Scripture, we are reminded of the difference between Christ, the living Word, and the letter of Scripture. We are told that this is the very way to exalt Scripture, when we own it to be the faithful and only direction to Him who is the true Light of men. Just as the highest honour a disciple of John the Baptist could confer on his teacher was to leave him and go to Christ, so the Scriptures, the more we study and rejoice in them, will only have their full effect upon us, as they daily point us away to Christ. They can awaken us to desire and obedience and diligence and faith; it is Christ Himself whom faith receives, who becomes within us the Life and the Light of our souls.

Blessed is the man who uses diligently the means of

grace and submits faithfully to all the teaching of the
word, and gratefully accepts all the refreshings of his
minority as a training for the life and the work of his
spiritual manhood. Let us use all outward instruction
as the guide to that which it ever points to—the birth of
the Spirit of Love within us.

There is a solemn and very urgent need of applying
all this to our daily Bible-reading, and to all the preaching we hear. It is possible to be most diligent, and even
successful in our Bible study, and yet to miss the real
blessing it is meant to bring. Scripture ever points us
away from itself to the Living Word, Christ Jesus, who
waits to be formed within us, and to the Blessed Spirit
who is within us, and is alone able to make what we read
or hear "truth in the inward part." The Holy Spirit,
by whose inspiration the Word was written, and by
whose inspiration alone the Word can become life within
us, who, as the Spirit of Truth, is Himself the Truth,
the Power, the Life of all that is in the word, dwells
within you. Turn with each thought of Divine things,
with each word of God you would fain spiritually apprehend, turn inward and wait quietly, in the faith that the
true Divine Teacher can make it true to you, can make
it live in you. Let your heart open to Him in the quiet
confession of the insufficiency of your understanding, in
the quiet faith of His hidden but sure and almighty
teaching. So will you find truth and grace, and all
goodness, not by human thought and feeling, but by
the birth and power of a Divine life within you, giving
you the very things, the actual realities of what the
word speaks of.

(reckon)

4. *The Inward Birth of Goodness in the Soul.*

Theophilus.—Now if you can show that the written word in the Bible can have any other or higher office or power than such a ministerial one as the Baptist had, I am ready to hear you.

Eusebius.—There is no possibility of doing that.

Theophilus.—But if that is not possible to be done, then you are come to the full proof of this point, viz., that there are two ways of attaining knowledge, goodness, virtue, &c., the one by the ministry of outward, verbal instruction, either by men or books, and the other by an inward birth of Divine light, goodness, and virtue in our own renewed spirit; and that the former is only in order to the latter, and of no benefit to us, but as it carries us farther than itself, to be united in heart and spirit with the Light, and Word, and Spirit of God. Just as the Baptist had been of no benefit to his disciples unless he had been their guide from himself to Christ.

But to come now closer to our subject in hand.

From this twofold light or teaching there necessarily arises a twofold state of virtue and goodness. For such as the teacher or teaching is, such is the state and manner of the goodness that can be had from it. Every effect must be according to the cause that produces it. If you learn virtue and goodness only from outward means, from men or books, you may be virtuous and good according to time, and place, and outward forms; you may do works of humility, works of love and benevolence, use times and forms of prayer; all this virtue and goodness is suitable to this kind of teaching, and may very well be had from it. But the spirit of prayer, the spirit of love, and the spirit of humility, or of any other virtue, are only to be attained by the operation of the light and Spirit of God, not outwardly teaching, but inwardly bringing forth a new-born spirit within us.

And now, let me tell you both that it is much to be feared that you as yet stand only under this outward teaching; your good works are only done under obedience to such rules, precepts, and doctrines as your reason assents to, but are not the fruits of a new-born spirit within you. But till you are thus renewed in the spirit of your minds, your virtues are only taught practices, and grafted upon a corrupt bottom. Everything you do will be a mixture of good and bad; your humility will help you to pride, your charity to others will give nourishment to your own self-love, and as your prayers increase, so will the opinion of your own sanctity. Because till the heart is purified to the bottom, and has felt the axe at the root of its evil (which cannot be done by outward instruction), everything that proceeds from it partakes of its impurity and corruption.

Now that Theogenes is only under the law, or outward instruction, is too plain from the complaint that he made of himself. For notwithstanding his progress in the doctrine of love, he finds all the passions of his corrupt nature still alive in him, and himself only altered in doctrine and opinion.

The same may be well suspected of you, Eusebius, who are so mistaken in the Spirit of Love that you fancy yourself to be wholly possessed of it, from no other ground but because you embrace it, as it were, with open arms, and think of nothing but living under the power of it. Whereas, if the Spirit of Love was really born in you from its own seed, you would account for its birth and power in you in quite another manner than you have here done; you would have known the price that you paid for it, and how many deaths you had suffered, before the Spirit of Love came to life in you.

Eusebius.—But surely, sir, imperfect as our virtues are, we may yet, I hope, be truly said to be in a state of grace; and if so, we are under something more than mere outward instruction. Besides, you very well know that it is a principle with both of us to expect all our goodness from the Spirit of God dwelling and working in us. We live in faith and hope of the Divine operation; and therefore I must needs say that your censure upon us seems to be more severe than just.

Theophilus.—Dear Eusebius, I censure neither of you, nor have I said one word by way of accusation. So far from it, that I love and approve the state you are both in. It is good and happy for Theogenes that he feels and confesses that his natural tempers are not yet subdued by doctrine and precept. It is good and happy for you also, that you are so highly delighted with the doctrine of love, for by this means each of you have your true preparation for further advancement. And though your state has this difference, yet the same error was common to both of you. You both of you thought you had as much of the

Spirit of Love as you could or ought to have ; and
therefore Theogenes wondered he had no more benefit
from it ; and you wondered that I should desire to
lead you farther into it.   And therefore, to deliver
you from this error, I have desired this conference
upon the practical ground of the Spirit of Love, that
you may neither of you lose the benefit of that good
state in which you stand.

Corresponding to the two ways of learning truth,
there is a twofold state of goodness.   The one in which
the Christian lives the mingled life, and everything he
does is a mixture of good and bad.   Life is one continued struggle between the flesh and the spirit, with
frequent failure, and continual ebb and flow in the
experience.   The other comes when, in the renewed
spirit, there is accomplished that inward birth for which
it has longed and struggled, and, by the Spirit of God
becoming the spirit of our life, the very spirit of humility, of love, of prayer, lives and works in us.
Theophilus feels it of such consequence that his
friends should make no mistake here, that he deals
with the utmost faithfulness, and plainly tells them that
he fears that, while they are enamoured of what they
have heard of the Spirit of Love, they are still very
much in the lower stages of hearing and understanding
and enjoying the teaching concerning Divine love, without possessing it.   The one, notwithstanding his progress
in the doctrine of love, finds all the passions of his corrupt
nature still alive in him, and himself only altered in
doctrine and opinion.   The other fancies himself to be
possessed by it because of his delight in it, while he shows

that he knows nothing of the price to be paid by a man before the Spirit of Love comes to life in him.

Let us allow Law to deal as personally with ourselves.

All profit to be derived from his teaching on the Spirit of Love, all real advance toward what Scripture calls the life of the spiritual man, or the perfect man, the man of full age, will depend upon our honest admission of the imperfection, not only of our present attainments—all are willing to admit that—but of our spiritual state, and the clear apprehension of that true Spirit of Love in which God actually desires, and has made provision, that we should live.

The analogy of our human birth may help us to understand the teaching. The object of every human birth is a full-grown man. This object is not attained at birth. Because a man, with the help of his parents, is to have the making of himself, he comes into the world as a babe, who is to grow and learn, to be trained and exercised, and so to reach manhood with his powers fully prepared to take his place as a man. It is only as he enters upon manhood that the object of the birth is attained. Even so in the Christian life, regeneration makes a man a child of God, but a child who is, through much training and struggling, to grow up into a manhood in which he "attains unto a full-grown man, unto the measure of the stature of the fulness of Christ." It is then only that the Holy Spirit attains His purpose, and fills him, so as to be within him the spirit of all his life. Then it is that love can indeed be the law of all his being. The privilege and mark of a child is, being loved and helped. The privilege and mark of a man is the power of loving and caring for others.

5. *The Full Birth of the Spirit of Love.*

Eusebius.—Pray, therefore, proceed as you please. For we have nothing so much at heart as to have the truth and purity of this Divine love brought forth in us. For as it is the highest perfection that I adore in God, so I can neither wish nor desire anything for myself but to be totally governed by it. I could as willingly consent to lose all my being as to find the power of love lost in my soul. Neither doctrine, nor mystery, nor precept has any delight for me, but as it calls forth the birth, and growth, and exercise of that Spirit, which doth all that it doth, towards God and man, under the one law of love. Whatever, therefore, you can say to me, either to increase the power, manifest the defects, or remove the impediments of Divine love in my soul, will be heartily welcome to me.

Theophilus.—I apprehend that you do not yet know what Divine love is in itself, nor what is its nature and power in the soul of man. For Divine love is perfect peace and joy; it is a freedom from all disquiet, it is all content and mere happiness, and makes everything to rejoice in itself. Love is the Christ of God; wherever it comes, it comes as the blessing and happiness of every natural life, as the restorer of every lost perfection, a redeemer from all evil, a fulfiller of all righteousness, and a peace of God which passeth all understanding. Through all the universe of things, nothing is uneasy, unsatisfied, or restless, but because it is not governed by love, or because its nature has not reached or attained the

full birth of the Spirit of Love. For when that is
done, every hunger is satisfied, and all complain-
ing, murmuring, accusing, resenting, revenging, and
striving are as totally suppressed and overcome, as
the coldness, thickness, and horror of darkness are
suppressed and overcome by the breaking forth of
the light. If you ask why the Spirit of Love cannot
be displeased, cannot be disappointed, cannot complain, accuse, resent, or murmur, it is because Divine
love desires nothing but itself; it is its own good,
it has all when it has itself, because nothing is good
but itself and its own working; for love is God,
"and he that dwelleth in God, dwelleth in love."
Tell me now, Eusebius, are you thus blessed in the
Spirit of Love?

Read over again the first paragraph of the above
passage, and see the spirit in which an inquirer should
seek to have the truth of Divine love brought forth in
him. It is all comprised in this: "As it is the highest
perfection in God, I desire nothing but to be totally
governed by it. I could as willingly consent to lose
my whole being as to find the power of love lost in my
soul."—May God help us to say so too.

And yet Theophilus says: "I apprehend that you
do not yet know what Divine love is in itself, nor what is
its nature and power in the soul of man." Read the
two sentences that then follow as his description of
what love is in the soul of man.

And now, as to its nature and power in the soul of
man, everything is contained in the expression—*the full
birth of the Spirit of Love.* Regeneration is a Divine

birth, in which the Christian becomes a babe in Christ.
The full outbirth of that beginning is, as we saw, when
he has been taught to know what God means him to
be, and has intelligently and with his whole heart given
himself to be possessed by God's Holy Spirit and to be
filled with His love.

We all know what a birth is. It is the commence-
ment of a life, with an innate power of acting out all
its functions. Life may be feeble or sickly, but when
healthy and mature, the exercise of every function is a
joy. And so when a soul comes to the full birth of
the Spirit of Love, love is its life; to love becomes most
natural, the only thing it can do. The power it exerts
is not, as it was in the preparatory stage, that of effort
and strain with continual failure, but the power of an
endless life—a Divine operation of the Spirit of God
teaching and enabling to love. A loving nature cannot
help loving. Love can be hindered or kept from loving
by nothing. The more of opposition or ingratitude it
meets, the more opportunity for proving its Divine
nature and power. Love is its own happiness; it is a
joy to love. Nothing can interfere with the blessedness
of this Divine life in the soul. Its only desire is to pro-
pagate itself and become the blessing and happiness of
everything that wants it. It is, therefore, evident that
though the Spirit of God dwell in you, He has not
obtained the mastery, He has not become the Spirit
of your life, till you love freely and entirely according to it.

When our Lord Jesus, on the last night, gave the new
commandment to love just as He had loved, He did so
in connection with the promise of the coming baptism
of the Spirit. It is by the Holy Spirit filling the heart
that John's words come true and are understood: " He
that abideth in love, abideth in God and God in Him.

Hereby know we that we abide in Him and He in us, because He hath given us of His Spirit." Let us believe that the full birth of the Spirit of Love within us is our rightful heritage, that whoso keepeth His word, in him verily is the love of God perfected.

6. *Are you thus Blessed?*

Theophilus.—Tell me now, Eusebius, are you thus blessed in the Spirit of Love?

Eusebius.—Would you have me tell you that I am an angel, and without the infirmities of human flesh and blood?

Theophilus.—No; but I would have you judge of your state of love by these angelical tempers, and not by any fervour or heat that you find in yourself. For just so much and so far as you are freed from the folly of all earthly affections, from all disquiet, trouble, and complaint about this or that, just so much and so far is the Spirit of Love come to life in you. For Divine love is a new life and new nature, and introduces you into a new world; it puts an end to all your former opinions, notions, and tempers; it opens new senses in you, and makes you see high to be low, and low to be high, wisdom to be foolishness, and foolishness wisdom; it makes prosperity and adversity, praise and dispraise, to be equally nothing. "When I was a child (saith the Apostle), I thought as a child, I spake as a child; but when I became a man, I put away childish things." Whilst man is under the power of nature, governed only by worldly wisdom, his life (however old he may be) is quite childish; everything about him only awakens childish thoughts and pursuits in him; all that he sees and hears, all that he desires or fears, likes, or dislikes; that which he gets, and that which he loses; that which he hath, and that which he hath not, serve only to carry him from this fiction of evil to that fiction of good, from one vanity of peace to another vanity of trouble. But when **Divine love is born** in the soul, all childish images of good and evil are done away, and all the sensibility of them is lost, as the stars lose their visibility when the sun is risen.

" Tell me, Eusebius, are you thus blessed in the Spirit of Love?" The answer Eusebius gives is exactly that which most Christians would give. Are you not speaking of impossibilities? Your ideal is very beautiful, but unattainable. " Would you have me tell you that I am an angel, and without the infirmities of human flesh and blood?" The answer Theophilus returns is simple. " No, I do not expect you to be an angel, or free from the infirmities of flesh and blood. But I would not have you judge of your state of love by what you may at times feel, but by these heavenly tempers of which I have been speaking." Here is the great difference between two classes of Christians. The one is guided in its thoughts of the spiritual life and its own state by what it feels in its best moments to be within its reach. The other looks to God's Word, and the heavenly tempers of which it speaks, as both a possibility and an obligation, and makes that its rule of faith and prayer and conduct. The one makes its own thoughts of what is possible, the standard of desire and duty. The other asks only one thing—to know what the mind of God is, to have the vision of the pattern in the Mount, to find out exactly what *God expects His child to be according to the provision of grace and strength prepared in Christ and the Holy Spirit.* The former turns the question of Theophilus off with the thought, It is too high; the latter welcomes everything that can help to obtain to the very utmost what God can give and do.

Tell me now, Eusebius, are you thus blessed in the Spirit of Love? It will be well to read again the whole paragraph leading up to the question, and give the answer. And whether that answer be a simple No; or, It is what I have seen and am seeking after; or, In its blessed beginnings I have tasted of it; do let it bring us face to face with the fact that there is a fulness of love which God is willing to bestow, and which we do not yet enjoy, for no other reason than that we have not yet sought it with our whole heart. And let it just urge us to look more intently, and more wistfully, and more believingly at that full birth of the Spirit of Love come to life in us which we may count upon.

"Divine love is a new life and a new nature, and introduces you into a new world; it puts an end to all your former opinions, notions, and tempers." Study this till you feel that just as definitely as your regeneration was an act of God's almighty grace, so the perfecting of His work is equally the operation of Divine supernatural grace. The firmer the hold this truth gets on you, the more will you see the need of being brought away from all the life and lusts of the world, and the flesh and self, and of turning the whole heart heavenward to wait upon God Himself to give you this unspeakable blessing. Faith in Christ will get a new meaning to you in the hope of His indwelling in you with His temper and disposition; the power of the Holy Spirit will become to you as your daily bread, as your very breath from moment to moment, bringing fresh life and vigour into your system.

SECOND SECTION.

GOD IS LIGHT; SELF IS DARKNESS.

7. *The Dawning of the Light.*

Theogenes.—That this is the true power of the spirit of Divine love, I am fully convinced from my own uneasiness at finding that my natural tempers are not overcome by it. For whence could I have this trouble, but because that little dawning that I have of the Spirit of Love in me maketh just demands to be the one light, breath, and power of my life, and to have all that is within me overcome and governed by it. And therefore I find I must either silence this small voice of new risen love within me, or have no rest from complaints and self-condemnation, till my whole nature is brought into subjection to it.

Theophilus.—Most rightly judged, Theogenes; and now we are fairly brought to the one great practical point, on which all our proficiency in the Spirit of Love entirely depends, namely, that all that we are, and all that we have from Adam, as fallen, must be given up, absolutely denied and resisted, if the birth of Divine love is to be brought forth in us. For all that we are by nature is in full contrariety to this Divine love, nor can it be otherwise; a death to itself is its only cure, and nothing else can make it subservient to good; just as darkness cannot be altered, or made better in itself, or transmuted into light; it can only be subservient to the light by being lost in it and swallowed up by it.

Theogenes now begins to understand his position. He sees just the first dawning of the light of the Spirit of Love. He recognises that it is to this he owes the uneasiness and dissatisfaction with the present state of his heart and his temper. The sun has not yet risen upon him, but the dawn is the pledge of the sunrise. He has learnt to look upon that dawning as a call to let that love be the one light, power, and breath of his life, and to have all that is within him governed by it. Theophilus answers: "Most rightly judged; now we are come to the *one great practical point on which all our proficiency* in the Spirit of Love depends, namely, that all that we are, and all that we have from Adam, as fallen, must be given up, absolutely denied, if the birth of Divine love is to be brought forth in us. For all that we are is in full contrariety to this Divine love; *a death to itself is its only cure*, and nothing else can make it subservient to good."

This is the one lesson that Law reiterates with un-wearying assiduity. It is the one great condition Christ insisted on for every one who would come after Him: "Let him deny himself." That does not mean, deny and give up his sins, nor deny his own goodness, nor deny his own will and honour and pleasure. It means all that, but a great deal more too. Self means that life which is at the root of all our being and doing, the fountain whence it all issues, the power by which it acts. And it is the self-life that is to be denied if the life of Christ, if the Spirit of Love that is to enable us to live like God, and for God, only to bless others, is to possess us. " Because all our whole nature, as fallen from the life of God, is in a state of contrariety to the order and end of our creation; a continual source of disorderly appetites, corrupt tempers, and false judgments, therefore every motion of it is to be mortified, changed, and purified from its natural state, before we can enter the kingdom of God."

This denying of self is to be so entire, that it is to be a death to self, because all that we are by nature is in full contrariety to Divine love. It is only and alone in the death to self and the self-life that the Spirit of Love can enter and become our life; a death to itself is its only cure,'and nothing else can make it subservient to good—that means, that it is only when self has been given over to the death, and our life been freed from its rule, that man's will, and power, and energies can be made subservient to good, by becoming the humble, dependent, willing instruments of the Spirit of Love.

This expression brings Law to what he counts one of his clearest proofs, that in the very nature of things there is no other way to our being truly blessed but by a death to self preparing the way for the life of God. He says : " A death to itself is the only cure (of our nature), and nothing else can make it subservient to good. Just as darkness cannot be altered, or made better in itself, or transmuted into light, it can only be subservient to the light by being lost in it and swallowed up by it." He goes on to show how nature was in itself but darkness—a capacity for receiving and showing forth the light and the glory of God. And the whole of redemption aims at nothing less than this—discovering to us, and delivering us from the darkness of sin and self, restoring our nature to its true place as something that can be subservient to the light of God, by affording it a ground on which it could show forth all its glory.

8. *The Light of God.*

Theophilus.—All that we are by nature is in full contrariety to this Divine love, nor can it be otherwise; a death to itself is its only cure, and nothing else can make it subservient to good; just as darkness cannot be altered, or made better in itself, or transmuted into light, it can only be subservient to the light by being lost in it and swallowed up by it.

Now this was the first state of man; all the natural properties of his creaturely life were hid in God, united in God, and glorified by the life of God manifested in them; just as the nature and qualities of darkness are lost and hid when enlightened and glorified by the light. But when man fell from or died to the Divine life, all the natural properties of his creaturely life, having lost their union in and with God, broke forth in their own natural division, contrariety, and war against one another; just as the darkness, when it has lost the light, must show forth its own coldness, horror, and other uncomfortable qualities. And as darkness, though in the utmost contrariety to light, is yet absolutely necessary to it, and without which no manifestation or visibility of light could possibly be; so it is with the natural properties of the creaturely life; they are in themselves all contrariety to the Divine life, and yet the Divine life cannot be communicated but in them and by them.

Eusebius.—I never read or heard of the darkness being necessary to light; it has been generally considered as a negative thing, that was nothing in itself, and only signified an absence of light; but your doctrine not only supposes darkness to be something positive, that hath a strength and substantiality in itself, but also to be antecedent to the light, because necessary to bring it into manifestation. I am almost afraid to hear more of this doctrine; it sounds harsh to my ears.

Theophilus.—Don't be frighted, Eusebius. I will lead you into no doctrine but what is strictly conformable to the letter of Scripture and the most orthodox piety. The Scripture saith, "God is light, and in Him is no darkness at all;" therefore the Scripture affirmeth light to be superior, absolutely separate from, and eternally antecedent to darkness; and so do I. In this Scripture you have a noble and true account of light, what it is, where it is, and was, and always must be. It can never change its state or place, be altered in itself, be anywhere, or in another manner, than as it was, and will be, from and to all eternity. When God said, "Let there be light, and there was light," no change happened to eternal light itself, nor did any light then begin to be; but the darkness of this world then only began to receive a power or operation of the eternal light upon it, which it had not before; or eternity then began to open some resemblance of its own glory in the dark elements and shadows of time. And thus it is that I assert the priority and glory of light, and put all darkness under its feet, as impossible to be anything else but its footstool.

Eusebius.—I am quite delighted with this. But tell me now how it is that light can only be manifested in and by darkness.

Theophilus. —The Scripture saith that "God dwelleth in the light, to which no man can approach:" therefore the Scripture teacheth that light in itself is and must be invisible to man; that it cannot be approached or made manifest to him but in and by something that is not light. And this is all that I said, and the very same thing that I said, when I affirmed that light cannot be manifested, or have any visibility to created eyes, but in, and through, and by the darkness.

Light as it is in itself is only in the supernatural Deity; and that is the reason why no man or any created being can approach to it, or have any sensibility of it, as it is in itself. And yet no light can come into this world but that in which God dwelt before any world was created. No light can be in time but that which was the light of eternity. If, therefore, the supernatural light is to manifest something of its incomprehensible glory, and make itself, in some degree, sensible and visible to the creature, this supernatural light must enter into nature, it must put on materiality. Now darkness is the one only materiality of light in and through which it can become the object of creaturely eyes; and till there is darkness there is no possible medium or power through which the supernatural light can manifest something of itself, or have any of its glory visible to created eyes. And the reason why darkness can only be the materiality of light is this; it is because darkness is the one only ground of all nature and of all materiality, whether in heaven or on earth. And therefore everything that is creaturely in nature, that has any form, figure, or substance, from the highest angel in heaven to the lowest thing upon earth, hath all that it hath of figure, form, or substantiality only and solely from darkness. Look at the glittering glory of the diamond, and then you see the one medium through which the glory of the incomprehensible light can make some discovery or manifestation of itself.

All light, then, that is natural and visible to the creature, whether in heaven or on earth, is nothing else but so much darkness illuminated; and that which is called the materiality of light is only the materiality of darkness, in which the light incorporateth itself.

For light can be only that same invisible, unapproachable thing which it always was in God from all eternity; and that which is called the difference of light is only the difference of that darkness through which the light gives forth different manifestations of itself. It is the same whether it illuminates the air, water, a diamond, or any other materiality of darkness. It has no more materiality in itself when it enlightens the earth than when it enlightens the mind of an angel; when it gives colour to bodies than when it gives understanding to spirits.

God *is* light. Light is not only an image of what God is, but it is His very being and nature, and all earthly light is only an out-shining of His incomprehensible glory. All that light is to nature, God is to His creature. And in the pursuit of the Christian life, with its peace, its holiness, and its power, we shall never find anything higher or stronger, more blessed or more heavenly, than just letting the light of God shine in our hearts all the day. To illustrate and enforce this is the object of the present paragraph.

Theophilus first points out how nature was created, that in it the light of the glory of God might shine forth. As thought of separate from God, it is darkness, dependent on, and capable of receiving and reflecting, the Divine light. And just as all the nature and qualities of darkness are hid and swallowed up in the light, so all the natural properties of our creaturely life were filled with and glorified by the life and light of God manifested in them. God dwells in a light which is invisible and unapproachable. He can only be known as His light shines through and from those on whom He causes it to rest. So the light of the glory of God is seen in the face of Jesus Christ. And so it is seen too in the face and the life of His redeemed saints.

The thought that this suggests in regard to the blessedness of the Christian life and the pursuit of holiness is very wonderful indeed. We know how much light manifests its own beauty by the different objects on which it rests. The mountains and the clouds, trees and flowers and grass—all the beauties of shade and colour unite in showing the exceeding beauty of the light, to which alone they owe their beauty. Man was created that, just as nature reflects the glory of created light, so the exceeding glory of the uncreated light might be seen in us; and the redeemed soul can form no higher conception of its calling and blessedness than that of allowing God to shine into our heart, and to shine through us on the world around.

In the two closing paragraphs of this Dialogue, after having led us all the way through the death to self to the birth of the Spirit of Love, Law comes back to this as the sum and fulness of all blessing—the light of God in Christ rising in the soul, as it rises on heavenly beings (p. 101).

In restoring what has been broken down, it is a great help to get the original plan of the ruins we see. The study of what Adam was created for, as the bearer and reflector of the light of God, leads us to one of the highest and most helpful conceptions of the Christian life. The reality and intimacy of the Divine indwelling, the unceasing operation of the Divine power, the perfect rest and peace of the soul in God's keeping—this, the destiny of unfallen Adam, is now our heritage. Let us sink down in the consciousness of our emptiness and darkness, in trustful dependence upon the purpose and the power of God, and as the light of the morning, when the sun riseth, even as a morning without clouds, the light of God will rise upon us—God will shine in our hearts.

9. *Light is Power and Joy.*

Theophilus.—Sight and visibility is but one power of light, but light is all power; it is life, and every joyful sensibility of life is from it. "In Him (says the Apostle) was life, and the life was the light of men." Light is all things, and nothing. It is nothing, because it is supernatural; it is all things, because every good power and perfection of everything is from it. No joy or rejoicing in any creature, but from the power and joy of light. No meekness, benevolence, or goodness, in angel, man, or any creature, but where light is the lord of its life. Life itself begins no sooner, rises no higher, has no other glory, than as the light begins it and leads it on. Sounds have no softness, flowers and gums have no sweetness, plants and fruits have no growth, but as the mystery of light opens itself in them.

C

Whatever is delightful and ravishing, sublime and glorious, in spirits, minds, or bodies, either in heaven or on earth, is from the power of the supernatural light, opening its endless wonders in them. Hell has no misery, horror, or distraction, but because it has no communication with the supernatural light. And did not the supernatural light stream forth its blessings into this world, through the materiality of the sun, all outward nature would be full of the horror of hell.

And hence are all the mysteries and wonders of light, in this material system, so astonishingly great and unsearchable; it is because the natural light of this world is nothing else but the power and mystery of the supernatural light, breaking forth and opening itself, according to its omnipotence, in all the various forms of elementary darkness which constitute this temporary world.

Theogenes.—I could willingly hear you, Theophilus, on this subject till midnight, though it seems to lead us away from our proposed subject.

Theophilus.—Not so far out of the way, Theogenes as you may imagine; for darkness and light are the two natures that are in every man, and do all that is done in him.

The Scriptures, you know, make only this division, the works of darkness are sin, and they who walk in the light are the children of God. Therefore light and darkness do everything, whether good or evil, that is done in man.

Life and light are intimately connected. Light is at once the effect, the proof of life, and also its cause and support. To an extent we have little distinct conception of, all created life, animal as well as vegetable, depends upon it. From it life has its joy, its beauty, its wonders. And because all created light is only the manifestation of the light of eternity, of God who is light, there is no more fruitful and instructive type of the Divine life in man than the light.

And what is its chief lesson? Surely this, the silent but mighty power with which it does its quickening and gladdening work. As the trees and flowers share and bask in the sunshine, all the mysteries of growth and colour, of blossom and fruit, are gently but surely wrought out, to teach us that our chief need is to have our souls lie still in the light of God's presence, until it rests upon us as our unceasing joy and possession. At creation light came forth, because in it God would do all His work. In the light that each new morning brings, God continues and perfects His mighty work. In grace it is even so—the light of God's face and love shining on the soul is meant to be the very first condition of the further manifestation of His power to sanctify and make us fruitful. Let all who would learn the way to the full birth of the Spirit of Love in the soul, to which this book promises to lead them, be careful not to miss this lesson as they go along. The highest you can seek, the best you can obtain, can be nothing higher or better than this—the light of God rising on the soul and resting there. Begin with this at once, and carry it with you all along.

"For God, who commanded the light to shine out of darkness, hath shined in our hearts." That is the contrast to what precedes. "The god of this world hath blinded the minds of them which believe not, that the

light should not dawn upon them." There is nothing
darkens the hearts, even of God's children, so universally and so effectually, as the spirit of the world or
worldly-mindedness; seeking or delighting in the pleasures, the possessions, the pride, the wisdom of this
world. They cannot believe or receive this heavenly
invisible light of God shining in the heart. Let us
believe in it, and turn our hearts away from the world
heavenward to receive it. "God is light." It is His
very nature to shine; it is His very delight to shine in
our hearts.

That light of God shining in us is omnipotent. It will
give peace and brightness, joy and fruitfulness, purity
and wisdom. It will be as spring-time and summer to
our souls, giving fruitfulness and power to make glad
those around us. Above all, that light will reveal God
within us; in His light we shall see light. His holy
presence will dawn upon us as the morning. That
wonderful indwelling for which man was created, in
which God was to be and to do in him everything that
he did, will begin to be restored. Gentle and rest-
ful, penetrating and all-pervading, quickening and
blessing as the light, the glory of God in the face of
Jesus Christ will be the light that fills the soul.

10. *The Powers of Darkness.*

Theogenes. — What is this darkness in itself, or
where is it?

Theophilus. — It is everywhere, where there is nature
and creature. For all nature, and all that is natural
in the creature, is in itself nothing else but darkness,
whether it be in soul or body, in heaven or on earth.
And therefore, when the angels (though in heaven)
had lost the supernatural light, they became im-

prisoned in the chains of their own natural darkness.
If you ask why nature must be darkness, it is because
nature is not God, and therefore can have no light, as
it is nature.   For God and light are as inseparable as
God and unity are inseparable.   Everything, therefore, that is not God, is and can be nothing else in itself
but darkness; and can do nothing but in, and under,
and according to the nature and powers of darkness.

Theogenes.—What are the powers of darkness?

Theophilus.—The powers of darkness are the workings of nature or self: for nature, darkness, and self
are but three different expressions for one and the
same thing.

Now, every evil, wicked, wrathful, impure, unjust
thought, temper, passion, or imagination that ever
stirred or moved in any creature; every misery, dis-
content, distress, rage, horror, and torment that ever
plagued the life of fallen man or angel, are the very
things that you are to understand by the powers or
workings of darkness, nature, or self.   For nothing is
evil, wicked, or tormenting but that which nature or
self doth.

Theogenes.—But if nature is thus the seat and source
of all evil, if everything that is bad is in it and from
it, how can such a nature be brought forth by a God
who is all goodness?

Theophilus.—Nature has all evil, and no evil, in
itself.   Nature, as it comes forth from God, is darkness without any evil of darkness in it; for it is not
darkness without or separate from light, nor could it
ever have been known to have any quality of darkness
in it, had it not lost that state of light in which it

came forth from God, only as a manifestation of the goodness, virtues, and glories of light. Again, it is nature, viz., a strife and contrariety of properties for this only end, that the supernatural good might thereby come into sensibility, be known, found, and felt by its taking all the evil of strife and contrariety from them, and becoming the union, peace, and joy of them all. Nor could the evil of strife and contrariety of will ever have had a name in all the universe of nature and creature, had it all continued in that state in which it came forth from God. Lastly, it is self, viz., an own life, that so, through such an own life, the universal incomprehensible goodness, happiness, and perfections of the Deity might be possessed as properties and qualities of an own life in creaturely finite beings.

And thus, all that is called nature, darkness, or self has not only no evil in it, but is the only true ground of all possible good.

But when the intelligent creature turns from God to self, or nature, he acts unnaturally, he turns from all that which makes nature to be good; he finds nature only as it is in itself, and without God. And then it is that nature, or self, hath all evil in it. Nothing is to be had from it, or found in it, but the work and working of every kind of evil, baseness, misery, and torment, and the utmost contrariety to God and all goodness. And thus, also, you see the plainness and certainty of our assertion, that nature, or self, hath all evil, and no evil, in it.

In this passage Law gives us a remarkable and most suggestive interpretation of what darkness is, in its double contrast to the light of God. God is Light, all Light, alone Light; there is no light but in Him. The creature, therefore, and all nature, as brought forth by God, neither has, nor was it ever intended to have, light in itself. As regarded in itself, nature is nothing but darkness. But this darkness has no evil in it: it is a darkness of want or absence of light, but at the same time a capacity or fitness for receiving the light. But when the creature, first in the fallen angels, and then again in fallen man, turned from God to self, chose himself and his darkness instead of the light of God, darkness, with its dependence on God, lost its innocence, became evil, and the source of all evil. And just as fallen angels are bound in the chains of their own darkness and death, so darkness is the condition of everything on which the light of God does not shine.

The practical value of the truth here, where we are engaged in the pursuit of the full birth of the Spirit of Love, is very great. What our author wants to imprint upon us is the deep and irreconcilable contrariety between light and darkness, as the only true type of the distance between what is of God and what is of man. God created man with a self, an own life, with which he, as endowed with will, was to choose God, to take hold of, to receive, to be filled with all His will and blessedness. When man turned from God and chose the darkness, that darkness was no longer mere defect or absence of light, but, as inspired by self, the positive rejection of God. This self, or darkness, is now the power that animates and pervades the whole of human nature. As was said in a previous paragraph, it cannot be improved, or altered, or transmuted into light: a death to itself, an entire giving up of its own life, to

receive a supernatural life in the Light of God, is the
only hope of deliverance.

This contrast between light and darkness is meant to
show us that in man's nature there is nothing morally
indifferent—it is under the dominion of either of these
two powers. The powers of darkness, he says, are
nothing but the workings of nature or self. In the
discussion of what sin and holiness is, there is some-
times a desire to find out a neutral territory, in which
natural temperaments, and the actions proceeding from
them, have no special moral value. A true insight into
the origin, the nature, the power of evil, will show how
impossible this is; everything, however great or small,
belongs to the region of either light or darkness. As we
believe this, the deep humility, confession of impotence,
and sense of helpless dependence that becomes us; the
sinfulness of all that is not of God; the need of an actual
incoming of God, the Holy Ghost, to take entire charge
and possession; will prepare us for turning with our
whole heart to find our help in God alone.

11. *The Four Elements of Self.*

Theogenes.—I plainly enough perceive that nature,
or self, without God manifested in it, is all evil and
misery. But I would, if I could, more perfectly
understand the precise nature of self, or what it is
that makes it to be so full of evil and misery.

Theophilus.—Covetousness, envy, pride, and wrath
are the four elements of self, or nature, or hell, all of
them inseparable from it. And the reason why it
must be thus, and cannot be otherwise, is because
the natural life of the creature is brought forth for the
participation of some high, supernatural good in the

Creator. But it could have no fitness or possible capacity to receive such good, unless it was in itself both an extremity of want and an extremity of desire *(will)* of some high good. When, therefore, this natural life is deprived of or fallen from God, it can be nothing else in itself but an extremity of want continually desiring, and an extremity of desire continually wanting. And hence it is that its whole life can be nothing else but a plague and torment of covetousness, envy, pride, and wrath, all which is precisely nature, self, or hell.

Now covetousness, pride, and envy are not three different things, but only three different names for the restless workings of one and the same will or desire, which, as it differently torments itself, takes these different names, for nothing is in any of them but the working of a restless desire; and all this because the natural life of the creature can do nothing else but work as a desire. And therefore, when fallen from God, its three first births, and which are quite inseparable from it, are covetousness, envy, and pride; it must covet, because it is a desire proceeding from want; it must envy, because it is a desire turned to self; it must assume and arrogate, because it is a desire founded on a real want of exaltation, or a higher state.

Now wrath, which is a fourth birth from these three, can have no existence till some or all of these three are contradicted, or have something done to them that is contrary to their will; and then it is that wrath is necessarily born, and not till then.

And thus you see, in the highest degree of certainty, what nature or self is as to its essential constituent

Fallen State

want/desire → will

parts. It is the three fore-mentioned, inseparable
properties of a desire, thrown into a fourth of wrath
that can never cease, because their will can never be
gratified. For these four properties generate one
another, and therefore generate their own torment.
They have no outward cause nor any inward power
of altering themselves. And, therefore, all self, or
nature, must be in this state till some supernatural
good comes into it, or gets a birth in it. And, therefore, every pain or disorder in the mind or body of
any intelligent creature is an undeniable proof that
it is in a fallen state, and has lost that supernatural
good for which it was created. So certain a truth
is the fallen state of all mankind. And here lies the
absolute, indispensable necessity of the one Christian
redemption. Till fallen man is born again from
above, till such a supernatural birth is brought forth
in him, by the eternal Word and Spirit of God, he
can have no possible escape or deliverance from these
four elements of self or hell.

Whilst man, indeed, lives amongst the vanities of
time, his covetousness, envy, pride, and wrath may
be in a tolerable state, may help him to a mixture
of peace and trouble; they may have at times their
gratifications as well as their torments. But when
death has put an end to the vanity of all earthly
cheats, the soul that is not born again of the supernatural Word and Spirit of God must find itself
unavoidably devoured or shut up in its own insati-
able, unchangeable, self - tormenting covetousness,
envy, pride, and wrath. Oh, Theogenes, that I had
power from God to take those dreadful scales from

the eyes of every deist, which hinder him from seeing
and feeling the infinite importance of this most certain
truth !

We have seen in what the evil of self consists : that
self-life, which had been created to depend on God and
be made partaker of His goodness and glory, asserted
itself and turned from God and against God. Let us
now see what the forms are in which it manifests itself.
Law deduces them all from one root. The word desire
is one to which he everywhere attaches great importance,
as the first beginning and the great motive-power of all
life. God would not have created the world, would not
have begotten His Beloved Son, if it had not been for
desire. Coming from such a Creator, desire is the life-
principle of the creature. In all nature, animal and
rational, desire is the great motive-power of action.
Man was created to participate in the life, and the
goodness, and blessedness of his God. His fitness or
capacity to receive that good, was his sense of wanting
it, and his power of desiring it. In ever having that
desire satisfied in God would have been his blessedness.
In a sense of want continually desiring and desire continually wanting is the misery of man fallen from God.
On this account, the fallen creature can do nothing but
ever covet, a desire proceeding from the want of its true
good ; and ever envy, because it is a desire that has self
for its object ; and exalt itself, because it is a desire
reaching after a higher state than that in which it is.
Covetousness, envy, pride, are the three modes in which
one and the same restless desire ever manifests itself.
And out of these comes a fourth, the wrath or wretchedness
of unsatisfied desire. These four constitute the essential
elements of self. Amid the vanities and enjoyments of

time these desires may be partially gratified, and bring
a measure of peace or happiness; when these vanities
are removed, the soul finds itself devoured by an in-
satiable, never to be satisfied desire. It is only in the
Christian redemption, and by a birth of a new Divine
life in the soul through the Spirit of God, that man can
be delivered from self and its sins.

Let us see how we have here indeed all the elements
of the sin that robs us of our peace. Covetousness
is nothing but the incessant going out of our heart in
desire after what we may not or cannot have. Envy is
the cause of all the ill-will and resentment and unloving-
ness that disturbs us, because it cannot allow aught
to interfere with its own self-interest. And pride—sad
proof of our fall from something better than we are—
the seeking something higher than we possess, rebels
and exalts itself against all in God or man that will not
help to give us the place we seek. Altogether they often,
even in the Christian, work out a life of unrest and
despair.

This is the darkness of evil-self which the light of
God can cast out. But ere this can be done, the darkness must be confessed and turned from. The lust, and
the envy, and the pride of our nature, with the wretchedness they bring, must be acknowledged; and with that
our utter impotence to conquer them or cast them out.
The need must be felt of God's light to chase away the
darkness of self, of an entirely new life by the Holy
Spirit to take the place of the life of self, of an entire
death to self to make way for the birth of the Spirit of
Love from heaven.

Let us learn the lesson: the fuller the conviction
and confession of the darkness, *and its power*, the better
prepared we are for the shining of the light of God.

12. *The Malignant Nature of Self.*

Theogenes.—God give a blessing, Theophilus, to your good prayer. And then let me tell you that you have quite satisfied my question about the nature of self. I shall never forget it, nor can I ever possibly have any doubt of the truth of it.

You quite surprise me by thus showing me, with so much certainty, how the powers of eternity work in the things of time. Nothing is done on earth but by the unchangeable workings of the same spiritual powers, which work after the same manner both in heaven and in hell. I now sufficiently see how man stands in the midst of heaven and hell, under an absolute necessity of belonging wholly to the one or wholly to the other, as soon as this cover of materiality is taken off from him.

I now also see the full truth and certainty of what you said of the nature and power of divine love; viz., "that it is perfect peace and joy, a freedom from all disquiet, making everything to rejoice in itself. That it is the Christ of God, and wherever it comes, it comes as the blessing and happiness of every natural life; as the restorer of every lost perfection; a redeemer from all evil; a fulfiller of all righteousness; and a peace of God which passes all understanding." So that I am now a thousand times more than ever athirst after the Spirit of Love. I am willing to sell all, and buy it; its blessing is so great, and the want of it so dreadful a state, that I am even afraid of lying down in my bed, till every working power of my soul is given up to it, wholly possessed and governed by it.

Theophilus.—You have reason for all that you say, Theogenes, for were we truly affected with things as they are our real good, or real evil, we should be much more afraid of having the serpents of covetousness, envy, pride, and wrath, well nourished and kept alive within us, than of being shut up in a pest-house, or cast into a dungeon of venomous beasts.   On the other hand, we should look upon the lofty eloquence and proud virtue of a Cicero but as the blessing of storm and tempest, when compared with the heavenly tranquillity of that meek and lowly heart to which our Redeemer has called us.

I said the serpents of covetousness, envy, pride, and wrath, because they are alone the real, dreadful, original serpents ; and all earthly serpents are but transitory, partial, and weak out-births of them. All evil, earthly beasts are but short-lived images or creaturely eruptions of that hellish disorder that is broke out from the fallen spiritual world ; and by their manifold variety they show us that multiplicity of evil that lies in the womb of that abyss of dark rage which (*N.B.*) has no maker, but the three first properties of nature, fallen from God and working in their own darkness.

So that all evil, mischievous, ravenous, venomous beasts, though they have no life but what begins in and from this material world, and totally ends at the death of their bodies, yet have they no malignity in their earthly temporary nature, but from those same wrathful properties of fallen nature, which live and work in our eternal fallen souls. And, therefore, though they are as different from us as time from eternity, yet wherever we see them, we see so many infallible proofs of the fall of nature and the reality of hell. For, was there no hell broke out in spiritual nature, not only no evil beast, but no bestial life, could ever have come into existence.

But to return. I have, I hope, sufficiently opened unto you the malignant nature of that self which dwells in and makes up the working life of every creature that has lost its right state in God—viz., that all the evil that was in the first chaos of darkness, or that still is in hell and devils, all the evil that is in material nature and material creatures, whether animate or inanimate, is nothing else, works in and with nothing else, but those first properties of nature, which drive on the life of fallen man in covetousness, envy, pride, and wrath.

It is not enough that we know the elements of self, and are thus able to trace every sin to its true root. We need as much to study self as a whole, and to get a right impression of the essential and incurable evil of all that it is, and all that comes from it. What Law wants us to realise is, that as all goodness comes from God, and points to Him, so all evil, whether as we see it in venomous serpents, or in fallen spirits in hell, or in ourselves, has one origin—the darkness of nature separated from God. The serpents of covetousness, envy, pride, and wrath are the only real serpents, and our terror of harbouring them within us ought to be much greater than any fear we ever could feel of being cast into a dungeon full of venomous beasts.

How little this is believed or realised! And as a consequence, how little the blessing of being delivered from them, and of enjoying the heavenly tranquillity of the meek and lowly heart, is sought after! How many Christians there are, from whom the malignity of all that is of self is hid, and who oftentimes harbour and nourish the evil temper of pride, and envy, and worldliness, without any conception of what their real nature is.

If the redemption in Christ is to be appreciated, we need to know the depth of the fall from which it delivers us. We need to know the inherent evil of our own nature. We need to connect all the selfishness and anger, the pride and self-seeking, the desires of the world and the flesh, with their one root—self, turned from God and fallen under the power of the evil one. We need to study that root of evil within us in its oneness with the whole kingdom of darkness, with the power of Satan and the misery of hell, until our whole heart abhors it and seeks, above everything, for deliverance.

What a list of words there is in our language to express the various workings of this sinful self. Selfishness, self-assertion, self-confidence, self-pleasing, self-sufficiency, self-seeking. Our loathing of all these forms of sin will depend upon the measure in which we truly believe what we have been taught of self—that it is the power which was given us to turn to God and glorify Him, turned in pride from Him and against Him, and set on fire of hell to exalt itself against Him.

We have here our last lesson before we proceed to the great point of the Dialogue—the deliverance from self by the dying to it. The needs-be of such an entire deliverance, and at such a price, the desire to seek and obtain it at any price, will neither be understood nor felt, until we, in some measure, see that this self is indeed the very serpent that poisons our whole life, until we flee from it and cry for help to have it slain. Until this serpent, and all that is of the seed of the serpent, be known and hated, the Bruiser of the serpent cannot be known, or sought, or loved as He should be.

THIRD SECTION.

OF DYING TO SELF TO LIVE TO GOD.

13. *Death to Self not by Own Effort.*

Theogenes.—I could almost say that you have shown me more than enough of this monster self, though I would not be without this knowledge of it for half the world. But now, sir, what must I do to be saved from the mouth of this lion, for he is the depth of all subtlety, the Satan that deceiveth the whole world. He can hide himself under all forms of goodness, he can watch and fast, write and instruct, pray much and preach long, give alms to the poor, visit the sick, and yet often gets more life and strength, and a more unmoveable abode, in these forms of virtue, than he has in publicans and sinners.

Enjoin me, therefore, whatever you please ; all rules, methods, and practices will be welcome to me, if you judge them to be necessary in this matter.

Theophilus.—There is no need of a number of

D

practices or methods in this matter. For to die to self, or to come from under its power, is not, cannot be done by any active resistance we can make to it by the powers of nature. For nature can no more overcome or suppress itself than wrath can heal wrath. So long as nature acts, nothing but natural works are brought forth, and therefore the more labour of this kind, the more nature is fed and strengthened with its own food.

But the one true way of dying to self is most simple and plain; it wants no arts or methods, no cells, monasteries, or pilgrimages; it is equally practicable by everybody; it is always at hand; it meets you in everything; it is free from all deceit, and is never without success.

In this short passage there are two thoughts on which Law dwells repeatedly at length in his writings. The one, that self can hide himself under all forms of goodness, and gets a more unmoveable abode in these forms of virtue than he has in publicans and sinners. This thought ought to alarm us all. Self can watch and fast, pray much and preach long; self can become religious, take pleasure in its duties, and be exceeding diligent in its services. Law wants to lead us to dying to self, but this cannot be until we know what self is. If we do not know to seek him where he hides in his cloak of religion, all teaching and effort will be vain. We may be ready to die to his pride and sin, and not know that his stronghold is in the temple. Self will even offer to lead and to help us in dying to self. It is only when we begin so to fear his terrible subtlety as to give up all hope of discovering him and bringing him to execution, that we shall come to that <u>real dying to self</u> to which Law would fain bring us—a sense of our utter inability to deal with self, a giving up all hope of conquering him, the entire casting of ourselves, in utter despair, on God alone to do the work.

This is what, as a second thought, is more distinctly expressed in a following sentence: To die to self, to come from under its power, cannot be done by any active resistance we can make to it by the powers of nature. How much mortification of self there has been, both in what was external and what appeared more inward; how much of penance and penitence, of self-scourging and self-loathing, which was <u>nothing but the</u> <u>work of self!</u> It is only when the soul is brought to believe in its own entire and utter impotence to deal directly with this monster, that it will begin to get an insight into the absoluteness of the surrender to God, and the trust in Him, which is needed if He alone is to do the work for us and in us. Christ conquered sin by dying to it. We died in Him, and are, even as He, dead to it. As we live "always bearing about the dying of the Lord Jesus," bearing *His dying* in us, the dying to self will be real and true. <u>Nothing that we do</u> <u>ourselves can have any good in it, because it is self working in us.</u> The good in us is the work of God's Spirit, and it is all preparatory to that full death to self to which He seeks to bring us, and in which we are entirely yielded up to God to work all in us.

All the failures of the Christian life are owing to nothing but this one thing, that we seek to do in our own strength what God Himself by His Spirit alone can work in us. Let us weigh well Law's words: To die to self, to come from under its power, cannot be done by any active resistance we can make to it by the power of nature. To exchange the life of self for the life of God, to come out of the darkness of self into the light of God, is a work we cannot do. It is the man who ceases from self, who sees and accepts in the death of Christ his death to self, and his entrance into the life of God as a gift from heaven, on whom the light of God will rise.

14. *The One True and Immediate Way of Dying to Self.*

Theophilus.—If you ask what this one, true, simple, plain, immediate, and unerring way is, it is **the way of patience, meekness, humility, and resignation to God.** This is the truth and perfection of dying to self; it is nowhere else, nor possible to be in anything else, but in this state of heart.

Theogenes.—The excellency and perfection of these virtues I readily acknowledge; but alas! sir, how will this prove the way of overcoming self to be so simple, plain, immediate, and unerring as you speak of? For is it not the doctrine of almost all men and all books, and confirmed by our own woeful experience, that much length of time, and exercise, and variety of practices and methods are necessary, and scarce sufficient, to the attainment of any one of these four virtues?

Theophilus.—When Christ our Saviour was upon the earth, was there anything more simple, plain, immediate, unerring than the way to Him? Did scribes, pharisees, publicans, and sinners want any length of time or exercise of rules and methods before they could have admission to Him or have the benefit of faith in Him?

Theogenes.—I don't understand why you put this question, nor do I see how it can possibly relate to the matter before us.

Theophilus.—It not only relates to, but is the very heart and truth of the matter before us; it is not appealed to by way of illustration of our subject, but it is our subject itself, only set in a truer and stronger light. For when I refer you to **patience, meekness, humility, and resignation to God** as the one simple, plain, immediate, and unerring way of dying to self or being saved from it, I call it so for no other reason but because you can as easily and immediately, without art or method, by the mere turning and faith of your mind, have all the benefit of these virtues, as publicans and sinners by their turning to Christ, could be helped and saved by Him.

In the first sentence of the above passage you have a straight answer to the question, What is the true way of dying to self? How can a man be led to understand and desire and find what the death to sin and self in Christ gives him? It is the way of patience, meekness, humility, resignation to God. Dying to self, turning away and ceasing from it, refusing to be led by it, can be effected in no other way but just bowing low before God in the confession of sin and impotence, and the patient waiting for His work in us. The whole of the remainder of this Dialogue is devoted to the exposition and enforcing of this one lesson. He never wearies of repeating the expression: Patience, meekness, humility, and resignation to God; in what remains of the Dialogue it occurs some thirty times.

Here you have the truth and perfection of dying to self; it is in this state of heart alone that it is to be found.

Some will be in danger of thinking this advice too simple: how can these simple virtues of humility and meekness bring this high attainment—the death of self? Others will think the prescription beyond their reach—they think they need the death to self before they can be humble and meek. Let me beg of all to be patient; as they go on they will see how, if the death to self be for sinners such as we, and if it is to be wrought in us by the operation of God, the only possible way to it must just be our sinking down into our own helplessness, and humbly and patiently resigning ourselves to God, to work it in us.

And note especially, ere you leave the passage, what is said about the way of dying to self being one that brings immediate deliverance. If you look back to the first section, you will remember what we found there of two ways of seeking goodness, and a twofold state of goodness, the one of promise and preparation, the other of fulfilment and possession. When Law speaks of the certain and immediate help which Christ can give in this matter, he does so because he knows that this is the best way for wakening desire, and drawing us on in that path of preparation which leads to the full birth of the Spirit of Love. He does so because he is going to point us to a Saviour who still says, " If thou canst believe, all things are possible to him that believeth;" to a Saviour who, in His infinite power, waits to impart to us all that He won for us by His death to sin and His being made alive unto God. Nothing will so help to awaken strong and urgent desire for deliverance from self; to convince of the sin of our unbelief, as the great hindrance in the way; to steady and strengthen our aim

after nothing less than just such immediate and definite
help as Christ gave to those who came to Him on earth;
or to see that we can come to Christ now in the same
simplicity of faith, and the same assurance of help, as
once brought the sick and the blind to Him.

Let us learn, whatever our experience be of the power
of self, in its sin or its impotence to conquer sin, in its
open outbreaks or its hidden power, to see that here is
the only cure—at once gently to sink down before God
in a humility that confesses its nothingness; in the
meekness that bows under and quietly bears the shame
we feel: in a patience that waits God's sure deliverance;
and a resignation that gives itself entirely to His will,
and power, and mercy. As easily and immediately as
sinners, by turning to Christ, were saved by Him, will
you, by the turning of your heart to them, receive the
blessed rest they bring.

15. *The Simplicity of Faith.*

Theogenes.—But, good sir, would you have me then
believe that my turning and giving up myself to these
virtues is as certain and immediate a way of my being
directly possessed and blessed by their good power
as when sinners turned to Christ to be helped and
saved by Him. Surely this is too short a way, and
has too much of miracle in it, to be now expected.

Theophilus.—I would have you strictly to believe
all this, in the fullest sense of the words. And also
to believe that the reasons why you, or any one else,
are for a long time vainly endeavouring after, and
hardly ever attaining, these first-rate virtues, is because you seek them in the way they are not to be

found, in a multiplicity of human rules, methods, and
contrivances, and not in that simplicity of faith in
which those who applied to Christ immediately obtained that which they asked of Him.

" Come unto Me, all ye that labour and are heavy
laden, and I will refresh you." How short, and
simple, and certain a way to peace and comfort, from
the misery and burden of sin ! What becomes now
of your length of time, and exercise, your rules, and
methods, and roundabout ways, to be delivered from
self, the power of sin, and find the redeeming power
and virtue of Christ ? Will you say that turning to
Christ in faith was once indeed the way for Jews and
heathens to enter into life, and be delivered from the
power of their sins, but that all this happiness was at
an end as soon as Pontius Pilate had nailed this good
Redeemer to the cross, and so broke off all immediate
union and communion between faith and Christ ?

What a folly would it be to suppose that Christ,
after His having finished His great work, overcome
death, ascended into heaven, with all power in heaven
and on earth, was become less a Saviour, and gave
less certain and immediate help to those that by faith
turn to Him now, than when He was clothed with
the infirmity of our flesh and blood upon earth ?
Has He less power, after He has conquered, than
whilst He was only resisting and fighting with our
enemies ? Or has He less good will to assist His
Church, His own body, now He is in heaven, than
He had to assist publicans, sinners, and heathens,
before He was glorified as the Redeemer of the
world ? And yet this must be the case, if our simply

turning to Him in faith and hope is not as sure a way
of obtaining immediate assistance from Him now as
when He was upon earth.

———

When Christ was upon earth, nothing was more
simple, plain, immediate, and certain than the way
of coming to Him. There was no length of time, no
multiplicity of rules or methods to be observed: all who
came in the simplicity and the humility of a faith that
knew it could not help itself, and turned from itself to
Him, found immediate access and relief. And now that
Christ is in heaven, and has taken His place on the
throne of grace, there has been no change in the way
to come to Him: now that we cannot see Him, more
than ever the way to Him, and to be helped by Him, is
a way of faith. Faith in Him can bring an immediate
and effectual deliverance from self. When He was
upon earth, the miracles that He wrought were for the
most part wrought on the body. Now that He has
been glorified in heaven, and received from the Father
the wondrous gift of "all power in heaven and on
earth," He waits to work far greater miracles in them
who can believe in them. The otherwise altogether
incurable disease of the soul, the dominion of self, from
this He can deliver them that trust Him for it. So far
from His exaltation to the throne having rendered
His help less sure, or less accessible, or less free for
our faith to claim, it calls us to a confidence and assurance such as those who were with Him never could have
had. Read the third paragraph of the above extract
over again, and let your heart be strengthened with
the faith that He who is mighty to save can heal your
disease, and that faith in Him is the one simple, only,
and immediate way to obtain it.

✗✗

✗✗

Only, let there be no wrong conception of the way in which this healing of your great disease is to come. Many would fain have that it should come by the death and entire removal of self. This is not the way. The death of self is something very different from the death to self which God's Word holds out to you. When Jesus died to sin, He did not slay sin in the sense of killing and annihilating it. No, sin is still living and reigning in all who submit to it, whether willingly or reluctantly. He died to it so that it had no power more to tempt or persecute Him. You are partakers of His death to sin, and to self, in which sin works; and the healing of your disease which He now gives is the power of His death to sin, and His living unto God, in such a way that He frees you from the dominion of self, so that you live in Him and His life, dead to it. As sure as those who believed in Him were healed of whatever disease they had, so surely does He still give healing to those who have the courage to trust Him for this wonderful blessing.

And now, whether it be that you have accepted this Divine gift of deliverance, and now still need to have opened up to you what it implies, and how you can stand in its full enjoyment ; or that you are longing for some insight into it, and the way to possess it ; turn at once, even this moment, to Christ, as the one only and most certain Deliverer from the power of self.

16. *This Way of Dying to Self the very Perfection of Faith.*

Theogenes.—You seem, sir, to me to have stepped aside from the point in question, which was not, whether my turning or giving myself up to Christ

Death of Self
Death to Self

in faith in Him, would not do me as much good
as it did to them who turned to Him when He was
upon earth? but whether my turning in faith and
desire, to patience, meekness, humility, and resignation to God, would do all that as fully for me now
as faith in Christ did for those who became His
disciples?

Theophilus.—I have stuck closely, my friend, to
the point before us. Let it be supposed that I had
given you a form of prayer in these words: "O
Lamb of God, that takest away the sins of the world;
or, O Thou bread that camest down from heaven; or,
O Thou that art the resurrection and the life, the light
and peace of all holy souls, help me to a living faith
in Thee." Would you say that this was not a prayer
of faith in and to Christ, because it did not call Him
Jesus or the Son of God? Answer me plainly.

Theogenes.—What can I answer you, but that this
is a most true and good prayer to Jesus, the Son
of the living God? For who else but He was the
Lamb of God, and the bread that came down?

Theophilus.—Well answered, my friend. When,
therefore, I exhort you to give up yourself in faith
and hope, to patience, meekness, humility, and
resignation to God, what else do I do but turn you
directly to so much faith and hope in the true Lamb
of God? For if I ask you what the Lamb of God is
and means, must you not tell me that it is and means
the perfection of patience, meekness, humility, and
resignation to God? Can you say it is either more
or less than this? Must you not therefore say that a
faith of hunger, and thirst, and desire of these virtues

is in spirit and truth the one very same thing as a faith of hunger, and thirst, and desire of salvation through the Lamb of God? And, consequently, that every sincere wish and desire, every inward inclination of your heart, that presses after these virtues, and longs to be governed by them, is an immediate, direct application to Christ, is worshipping and falling down before Him, is giving up yourself unto Him, and the very perfection of faith in Him.

Theogenes asks Theophilus whether he has not changed his line of argument when, for the expression, turning in faith and desire to patience, meekness, humility, and resignation to God, he substituted that of faith in Christ. Theophilus answers that he had changed the expression of set purpose. What is Christ, the Lamb of God, he asks, but the very embodiment of humility, meekness, patience, and resignation to God? These were the virtues which constituted Him the Lamb of God, which gave worth to His sufferings, which worked out our salvation, and form a most important part of them; how can any one desire or receive Christ truly without desiring and receiving these virtues? It is only the heart that really sees them to be the very nature and glory and life of the Lamb of God, that desires them, and turns to Him for them, that can really believe on and receive Him unto salvation.

It was great wisdom in Law thus first to put these virtues, in which dying to self actually consists, and then afterwards lead up to the Lamb of God, in whom they are to be found. How many Christians there are who seek after and trust in a suffering

Christ as their atoning Lamb, but who have never sought or accepted the meek and lowly Lamb of God in the moral glory of His Lamb nature to be their life. And yet this is the salvation God offers. The blood of the Lamb has rent the veil, and brought us nigh to God, that now we might be followers of the Lamb, and He lead us in the path in which He walked, in the very dispositions and tempers which made Him well-pleasing to God. He could never have died to sin had it not been for His humility, meekness, patience, and resignation to God. And He cannot possibly make us actually partakers of that blessed death to sin in any way other than by leading us, in meekness and lowliness, to forsake self, and give up ourselves to God as His own, as He did. In conscious helplessness, as often as self would assert itself, at once to sink down in humility, meekness, patience, and resignation to God is the very perfection of faith, and at the same time the very perfection of dying to self.

It is this true faith in the Lamb of God that brings us immediate help, as did the faith of the sufferers who came to Him on earth. In one aspect there is indeed a great difference. The bodily healing was something that was given once for all, and rendered a man independent of Christ. He might go and forget Him. The spiritual healing is something infinitely more blessed; it renders a man for every moment dependent on the unceasing immediate contact with his Redeemer. This need, however, of ever-renewed communication of health does not make the fact of the healing less immediate or less certain. The very moment the soul lets go itself and its strength, and sinks down in its nothingness into the humility and meekness of Christ, it is at once made whole. His humility and meekness become our life and our hope and our rest. And if we

learn to tarry there in the power with which the Lamb
will keep those who trust Him, in the power of the
death which He died at Jerusalem, the rest will be
abiding.

17. "*Learn of Me : I am meek and lowly of heart.*"

Theophilus.—If you distrust my words, hear the
words of Christ Himself: "Learn of Me (says He),
for I am meek and lowly of heart ; and ye shall find
rest unto your souls." Here you have the plain truth
of our two points fully asserted—*first*, that to be given
up to, or stand in a desire of patience, meekness,
humility, and resignation to God, is strictly the same
thing as to learn of Christ, or to have faith in Him.
Secondly, that this is the one simple, short, and infallible way to overcome or be delivered from all the
malignity and burden of self expressed in these words,
"And ye shall find rest unto your souls."

And all this because this simple tendency or inward inclination of your heart to sink down into
patience, meekness, humility, and resignation to
God, is truly giving up all that you are and all that
you have from fallen Adam ; it is perfectly leaving all
that you have, to follow and be with Christ ; it is your
highest act of faith in Him, and love of Him, the most
ardent and earnest declaration of your cleaving to Him
with all your heart, and seeking for no salvation but
in Him and from Him.   And, therefore, all the good
and blessing, pardon and deliverance from sin, that
ever happened to any one from any kind or degree of

faith and hope and application to Christ, is sure to be had from this state of heart, which stands continually turned to Him in a hunger and desire of being led and governed by His spirit of patience, meekness, humility, and resignation to God.

Oh, Theogenes, could I help you to perceive or feel what a good there is in this state of heart, you would desire it with more eagerness than the thirsty hart desireth the water-brooks; you would think of nothing, desire nothing, but constantly to live in it. It is a security from all evil and all delusion; no difficulty or trial, either of body or mind, no temptation, either within you or without you, but what has its full remedy in this state of heart. You have no questions to ask of anybody, no new way that you need inquire after, no oracle that you need to consult; for whilst you shut up yourself, in patience, meekness, humility, and resignation to God, you are in the very arms of Christ, your whole heart is His dwelling-place, and He lives and works in you, as certainly as He lived in and governed that body and soul which He took from the Virgin Mary.

When Christ called the weary to come to Him and said He would give them rest, He added, "Learn of Me, for I am meek and lowly of heart, and ye shall find rest to your souls." There is a difference between His giving the rest and our finding it. A child asks me if he may have money for something he wishes to buy. I consent, and tell him where he can find it in my study. He goes, and returns saying he cannot find it. He had

not listened properly to my directions, and so the money
I had consented to give he did not find. There are
many who come to Christ for rest, and yet never find
that perfect rest He promised. The reason is, they do
not learn of Him as the meek and lowly One. All our
unrest comes from self. When we learn in meekness to
bow before what God or man does to us, all our unrest
is gone at once ; Christ, the meek and lowly One, and
His meekness in our heart, give perfect rest.

"I am meek and lowly of heart." With these words
Christ tells us wherein His power of giving rest, and of
saving us from the unrest of sin consists. His meekness is His power to save, is the salvation He gives.
Learning of Him means learning to be meek and lowly
like Him. Self is proud, and refuses to bow to God ; to
bow in meekness before God with Christ, like Christ, in
Christ, is the sure and only way of being delivered from
self. Let us even now, at once, thus come to Christ,
and begin to learn of Him. Let every discovery of
what self is and does be met at once by this our only
hope—learning of Jesus, the meek and lowly One.

Note especially in the above passage the sentence in
the second paragraph, "The inward inclination of your
heart to sink down into patience, meekness, humility,
and resignation to God is truly giving up all that you
are, and all that you have, from fallen Adam ; it is perfectly leaving all that you have to follow and be with
Christ." The whole blessedness of our salvation consists in our being saved from ourselves, and what we are
through Adam. No exertions or performances of our
own can do anything in the least to free us from ourselves or to destroy self. What other way can there
then be to the death to self but the humble, patient
yielding ourselves to God to take possession of us, and
to work in us. When Christ died upon the Cross, what

was that death as a death to sin but a meek, patient,
humble yielding of Himself to God's will and into God's
hands, counting on Him to raise Him again? And what
can possibly be our death to sin, our participation in
Christ's death, our death to self, but the same sinking
down before God and abiding and living before Him in
that meek and patient resignation, which leaves all to
Him to work, which confidently depends and patiently
waits upon him.

No wonder Theophilus cries out, "O Theogenes,
could I help you to perceive or feel what a good there
is in this state of heart, you would desire it with more
eagerness than the thirsty hart desireth the water-brooks.
You would think of nothing, desire nothing, but constantly to live in it."

18. *Follow this Christ.*

Theophilus.—Learn whatever else you will from
men and books, or even from Christ Himself, besides
or without these virtues, and you are only a poor
wanderer in a barren wilderness, where no water of
life is to be found. For **Christ is nowhere but in
these virtues**; and where they are, there is He in
His own kingdom. From morning to night let this
be the Christ that you follow, and then you will fully
escape all the religious delusions that are in the world,
and, what is more, all the delusions of your own
selfish heart.

For to seek to be saved by **patience, meekness,
humility of heart, and resignation to God**, is truly
coming to God through Christ; and when these tempers live and abide in you, as the spirit and aim of
your life, then Christ is in you of a truth, and the life

E

that you then lead is not yours, but Christ that liveth
in you. For this is following Christ with all your
power; you cannot possibly make more haste after
Him, you have no other way of walking as He walked,
no other way of being like Him, of truly believing in
Him, of showing your trust in Him and dependence
upon Him, but by wholly giving up yourself to that
which He was, viz., to patience, meekness, humility,
and resignation to God.

There are many Christs, even among believers. Some
one aspect of His work or person is laid hold of and held
up to the neglect of others. Let us see whether this
Christ, in His humility and meekness, and entire devotion to God, is the Christ we trust in and desire after to
live and rule in our hearts, and whether the likeness to
Him in this is the salvation we seek. Think often of the
great truths which prove this humility of Christ to be
indeed the very salvation we need, the only salvation we
can find. When God created man, to find his blessedness in entire dependence upon Him, and in receiving
all life and goodness each moment from Him, humility
was the one condition of his continuing in that blessed
state. When man disobeyed and fell it was self-exaltation
that drew him from God, and became the ruling power
of his life, and the cause of all sin and wretchedness.
When Christ became man it was to restore in humanity
that blessed dependence upon God: by His humble, meek,
patient resignation to God to atone for our sin and create
anew in us the nature of man before the fall. And so it
is not only in the very nature of things that a humble
resignation to God is the only way of dying to self, but
it is the only salvation Christ has to give, and the only

way of being partaker of His death and life. Therefore, "From morning to night, let this be the Christ you follow."

From morning to night—you want to begin every day very definitely with an Act of Humility, recognising it as the first duty of the day and of your life to get into the right place of dependence before God, in meek, patient, humble resignation to Him. From morning to night—you need to see that it is not only in your morning devotions, when you ask and expect strength for the day, but through the whole day, for every moment of it, that the clothing of humility is to be worn. Many Christians are seeking the death to self as an attainment in the power of which they can work successfully, and regard the meek and humble resignation to God only as the gate or passage through which they enter upon this state. They don't understand that this meekness and lowliness of heart is to be the permanent state of heart in which alone the death to self can be maintained, as much as it was the state in which Christ always lived. The meek and lowly heart was the very root and essence of Christ's being and breathing all the way; it is to be ours too. From morning to night, uninterruptedly and unceasingly, let this be the Christ you follow.

19. Of Covetousness.

Tell me now, have I enough proved to you the short, simple, and certain way of destroying that body of self which lives and works in the four elements of covetousness, envy, pride, and wrath?

Theogenes.—Enough of all reason. But as to covetousness, I thank God I cannot charge myself with it; it has no power over me—nay, I naturally abhor it. And I also now clearly see why I have been so long struggling in vain against other selfish tempers.

Theophilus.—Permit me, my friend, to remove your mistake. Had covetousness no power over you, you could have no other selfish tempers to struggle against. They are all dead as soon as covetousness has done working in you. You take covetousness to relate only to the wealth of this world. But this is but one single branch of it; its nature is as large as desire, and wherever selfish desire is, there is all the evil nature of covetousness.

Now envy, pride, hatred, or wrath can have no possibility of existence in you, but because there is some selfish desire alive in you that is not satisfied, not gratified, but resisted, or disappointed. And therefore so long as selfish tempers, whether of envy, uneasiness, complaint, pride, or wrath, are alive in you, you have the fullest proof that all these tempers are born and bred in and from your own covetousness; that is, from that same selfish bad desire which, when it is turned to the wealth of this world, is called covetousness. For all these four elements of self, or fallen nature, are tied together in one inseparable band, they mutually generate and are generated from one another; they have but one common life, and must all of them live or all die together. This may show you again the absolute necessity of our one simple and certain way of dying to self, and the absolute insufficiency of all human means whatever to effect it.

Theogenes congratulates himself that of the four elements of self, there is one at least of which he is free. Covetousness he has always abhorred. Of the other three he confesses that Theophilus has taught him the reason why he had been struggling so long in vain against his selfish tempers. He had never understood before how there is no way of conquering self but by dying to it, and how the only way of dying to it is to live ever in humility, meekness, patience, and resignation to God.

Theophilus takes occasion to point out a serious mistake, and so to warn us against what may prove a great danger. We remember how he formerly showed us that desire is the first and highest power in the life of the creature, the sure proof of man's Divine origin, with his wonderful capacity of desiring after God, of receiving Him, and being satisfied with Him. When sin mastered him, then desire was turned from God to self and the world, and all his sin and wretchedness consists in a ceaseless desire after that which is not God. We confine the word covetousness to this desire turned towards the world ; but it really includes all that desire for honour and self-pleasing which is the cause of envy and pride and every sin against love.

To understand this is of great importance. As we know that all the elements of self have one common root, and that, while some people appear more free from one form of it than others, there is in all the same root of evil, we shall feel the need of having the axe laid to the root of the tree. All the branches have one common life, and must all of them live or die together. It profits little to be freed from one form of sin ; dying to self, to all our own life, to have the new life of the Spirit of Love born in us is an absolute necessity.

Theogenes admitted that for lack of this knowledge all his struggling against his selfish tempers had been

vain. How many Christians there are for whom it
would be well to join with him in the confession. It is
right and needful to fight with individual sins and to
cultivate individual graces. But when this is rested on
as all that we can do, the mistake is fatal to success.
Every rising of sin, every attempt to resist and refuse
its allurement, must lead us afresh to remember what
the secret root of self is in which it has its strength, and
what the only way of being delivered from its power.
It is Jesus Christ who takes away sin. As sure and
immediate as was the power that went forth out of His
earthly life to any one who but touched the hem of His
garment, is the help that comes from His glorified life
in the power of God's throne into the spirit that trusts
Him. As a soul sinks down in humility, meekness,
patience, and resignation to God, it proves that it consents to the death of self as utterly sinful and impotent,
and sets its hope on Christ alone. No one can thus
persevere in the path of humiliation and self-emptying
without knowing that there is deliverance, and sooner
or later experiencing that the life of Christ does triumph
over the life of self and takes its place.

20. *Of Despair of Self.*

Theophilus.—For, consider only this, that to be
angry at our own anger, to be ashamed of our own
pride, and strongly resolve not to be weak, is the up-
shot of all human endeavours; and yet all this is
rather the life than the death of self. There is no
help but from a total despair of all human help.
When a man is brought to such an inward full conviction as to have no more hope from all human
means than he hopes to see with his hands, or hear

with his feet, then it is that he is truly prepared to
die to self; that is, to give up all thoughts of having
or doing anything that is good in any other way but
that of a meek, humble, patient, total resignation
of himself to God. All that we do before this conviction is in great ignorance of ourselves, and full
of weakness and impurity. Let our zeal be ever so
wonderful, yet if it begins sooner, or proceeds farther,
or to any other matter, or in any other way than as it
is led and guided by this conviction, it is full of delusion. No repentance, however long or laborious, is
conversion to God till it falls into this state. For
God must do all, or all is nothing. But God cannot
do all till all is expected from Him. And all is not
expected from Him till, by a true and good despair of
every human help, we have no hope, or trust, or
longing after anything but a patient, meek, humble,
total resignation to God.

Death to self means a total despair of self—that is,
to give up all thoughts of having or doing anything
that is good in any other way but that of a meek,
humble, patient, total resignation of ourselves to God.
All that we do in religion without this conviction is
in ignorance of what we are, and is often rather the life
than the death of self. When we are ashamed or
vexed at our own pride, it is simply because we expected
something better of ourselves. When we condemn
ourselves for having been angry, it is with the hope of
not doing so again. When we purpose not to sin, it
is in a secret hope that by our resolve, and strength of

will, we may be kept from it.   All this is the life of self.
What we need is, to be brought to the inward full conviction, that as little as we can see with our hands, can
we of ourselves conquer self or sin.   It is this alone will
bring us to that entire dependence upon God, and that
simple faith in Christ Jesus, through which the operation
of God's Spirit can proceed freely in us.

God must do all, or all is nothing.   God cannot do all
till all is expected from Him.   And all is not expected
from Him, till, by a true and good despair of every
human help, we have no hope, or trust, or longing after
anything, but a patient, meek, humble resignation of all
to God.   In these three simple sentences we have the
sum of Law's practical theology.   No true good but what
God works Himself.   In the Son and the Spirit, God has
again taken possession of man, to dwell and work in him
as before the fall.   The one thing God asks of man is
faith—that he expect all good from Him alone.   And
the one hindrance to a true and a full faith is, that
the meek, humble, patient, total resignation to God, to
His mercy and power, is so little known or sought.   It
is for the lack of this that self exercises such a mighty
malignant power in the believer and the Church.

In the believer.   Do let us take a firm hold of this
truth, that every failure in the Christian life, every
outbreak of evil temper, every disappointment because
our prayers and efforts appear to avail so little, is owing
to a secret trust we have placed in the power of self
within ; and that to be delivered from this power nothing will help, but in faith to embrace the Lamb of God
with His meekness and lowliness, and to wait before
Him in patient resignation to God.   That gives immediate help.   Persevering in that will make us conquerors.
He will bring the Spirit of Love to the birth in us.

In the Church.   Alas ! in its divisions, in its fellow-

ship with the world, in its worldly wisdom, in its pride,
men giving and accepting honour in so many of its
methods and measures, how much there is that painfully
proves that self still reigns within God's temple on earth.
In the city of God, the Lamb, Meekness, enthroned
in the glory of God, is the temple, and is the Light
thereof. Shall we not seek for ourselves, and all we can
reach, to labour and pray that the humility of Christ may
take the place of the pride of self? There is not one
grace Christ spake of so often during His earthly life as
humility. Let it become the one desire and mark of the
true believer. Then alone will the glory of God be seen
upon His Church as we bow in the dust at His feet.
Wait for all from Him alone, and give Him the glory.
Then will the life of self make way for the life of love,
and the life of God.

21. The State of the Heart.

Theophilus.—And now, my dear friends, I have
brought you to the very place for which I desired this
day's conversation; which was to set your feet upon
sure ground with regard to the Spirit of Love. For all
that variety of matters through which we have passed
has been only a variety of proofs that the Spirit of
Divine Love can have no place or possibility of birth
in any fallen creature till it wills and chooses to be
dead to all self, **in a patient, meek, humble resignation to the good power and mercy of God.**

And from **this state of heart** also it is that the spirit
of prayer is borne, which is the desire of the soul
turned to God. Stand therefore steadfastly in this
will, let nothing else enter into your mind, have no
other contrivance, but everywhere, and in everything,

HEART — thoughts — words — Action — habit — Character — Legacy

to nourish and keep up this state of heart, and then
your house is built upon a rock; you are safe from all
danger; the light of heaven and the love of God will
begin their work in you, will bless and sanctify every
power of your fallen soul, you will be in a readiness
for every kind of virtue and good work, and will know
what it is to be led by the Spirit of God.

Our Lord Jesus said more than once: "He that
humbleth himself shall be exalted." The humbling is
our part; the exaltation is God's work. It was so with
Christ. He humbled Himself; therefore God hath
highly exalted Him. As we desire, and follow after,
and seek a share in His humility on earth, we shall
partake of the spirit and power of His glorified life in
heaven; we shall enter with Him into the love of God.
It is in the man who seeks to stand unchangeably fixed
in the meekness, humility, patience, and resignation of
the Lamb of God upon earth, on whom He will rise as
the light of heaven; in whom He will give the full birth
of the Spirit of Love. After Christ had, for three years,
instructed His disciples in humility, He opened up to
them, in the last night, the secret of a love in their heart
like the love with which He had loved them. The
humility that has and seeks nothing of itself or for
itself, will be crowned from heaven with the Holy Spirit
and the fulness of love.

This humility is to be, not a thing of now and then,
not only an act repeated from time to time, when we
pray, or when we see self rising and asserting itself, but
a state of the heart, the constant and unceasing disposition in which we live and walk before God and men,

"Everywhere and in everything, nourish and keep up this state of heart; then your house is built upon a rock; the light and the love of God will begin their work in you, will bless and sanctify every power of your fallen soul." Put your trust in Christ Jesus, and learn of Him, the Author and Giver of all meekness and lowliness of heart. Let this be the Christ you receive into your heart; let this His meekness and lowliness be the salvation you receive through His death on the cross. For it is in this state of a heart, conformed to the likeness of Christ's heart, that God reveals and proves the power of His salvation.

There are many Christians who forget this. Some identify salvation with pardon of sin; others with sanctification; others with the glory of heaven. They do not understand that the first is only the entrance into it; the second its blessed fruit and proof; the third its full manifestation. Salvation itself is the life of God in the soul, that for which man was created, now restored in Christ Jesus. And the life of God in the soul can be possessed in no other way than as the heart receives the operation of God's Spirit, and the indwelling of Christ, and is thus filled with the fulness of God. And the indwelling of Christ can be ours in no possible way but as we have the mind that was in Him, as His humility and meekness live in us. Christ's Spirit and likeness can only be in us as far as it is in our heart: so only can it be ours. This state of the heart, wrought by the renewing and strengthening of the Spirit in the inner man; a turning from self to God; a sinking down with desire and faith into the humility and meekness of the Lamb of God, our Redeemer, is the one preparation for having the Spirit of Love born in us as the Spirit of our life.

22. *Of the Feeling of Impotence.*

Theogenes.—But, dear Theophilus, though I am so delighted with what you say that I am loth to stop you, yet permit me to mention a fear that rises up in me. Suppose I should find myself so overcome with my own darkness and selfish tempers as not to be able to sink from them into a sensibility of **this meek, humble, patient, full resignation to God**; what must I then do, or how shall I have the benefit of what you have taught me?

Theophilus.—You are then at the very time and place of receiving the fullest benefit from it, and practising it with the greatest advantage to yourself. For though this patient, meek resignation is to be exercised with regard to all outward things and occurrences of life, yet it chiefly respects our own inward state, the troubles, perplexities, weaknesses, and disorders of our own fallen souls. And to stand **turned to a patient, meek, humble resignation to God,** when your own impatience, wrath, pride, and irresignation attacks yourself, is a higher and more beneficial performance of this duty, than when you stand turned to meekness and patience when attacked by the pride, or wrath, or disorderly passions of other people. I say, **stand turned to this patient, humble resignation,** for this is your true performance of this duty at that time; and though you may have no comfortable sensibility of your performing it, yet in this state you may always have one full proof of the truth and reality of it; and that is, when you seek for help no other way, nor in anything else, neither from men nor books, but wholly leave and give up yourself to be helped by the mercy of God. And thus, be your state what it will, you may always have the full benefit of this short and sure way of resigning up yourself to God. And the greater the perplexity of your distress is, the nearer you are to the greatest and best relief, provided you have but patience to expect it all from God. For nothing brings you so near to Divine relief as the extremity of distress.

"Suppose I find myself so overcome by my own darkness and selfish temper, as not to be able to practise the full resignation to God, what am I to do? what good will the advice you give do me?" The question asked by Theogenes is one that will come to almost every one who earnestly seeks to walk in the way of dying to self. He will not be long before he feels that he has not in him the humility and meekness he longs for. A sense of his utter impotence casts him down. Instead of feeling meek and humble, he feels the darkness and selfishness of his old nature assert itself. The lesson, with its promised blessing of dying to self, fails us, and only leaves us further from humility and resignation than we were before.

Listen to the answer: Now is the very best time for testing the teaching you have received, and receiving the fullest benefit from it. It is not a question of the feelings, but of the will. In regard to the virtues in question, Law has used the expressions, "Giving up yourself to;" "Standing in a desire, longing after;" "Standing, turned to, patience, meekness, resignation." We are not at once to look within to feel whether we are meek and humble, or whether we feel able to sink down into humility, as we wish. "I say, stand turned to this patient, humble resignation, for that is wholly leaving and giving up yourself to be helped by the mercy of God."

In the path that leads to God through death to self, this is one of the most important lessons a Christian has to learn. We look within to our own feelings, either to what we feel we have attained of true humility and resignation, or to what we feel of power to sink down into it, and when we discover the opposite of what we long for, we lose hope and strength. Let every Christian learn that it is the will that is the ruling power; that it is the will by which God judges us; that it is the will in which faith has its strength; that it is the will to which the Holy Spirit is given to conquer.

The fact of our darkness and selfishness overcoming us, instead of keeping us back, must be our greatest inducement at once to sink down and resign ourselves to God. The desire to do so is accepted by God, and he who perseveres will soon prove that deliverance comes. Read again the two last sentences of the passage, and let your very darkness and helplessness ever bring you low before the God whose power and mercy are waiting to help you. Let no lack of feeling, no sense of coldness or sinfulness discourage you. The more helpless you feel, the greater reason for at once turning to Him who alone can take away sin. Humility is the first of all virtues before God; is the only thing that can put us in the way of being helped; and has a Divine promise of certain blessing.

23. Of the Divine Operation.

Theophilus.—And the greater the perplexity of your distress is, the nearer you are to the greatest and best relief, provided you have but patience to expect it

all from God. For nothing brings you so near to
divine relief as the extremity of distress. For the goodness of God hath no other name or nature, but the
helper of all that wants to be helped; and nothing
can possibly hinder your finding this goodness of God,
and every other gift and grace that you stand in need
of; nothing can hinder or delay it but your turning
from the only fountain of life and living water to some
cracked cistern of your own making; to this or that
method, opinion, division, or subdivision amongst
Christians, carnally expecting some mighty things,
either from Samaria or Jerusalem, Paul or Apollos,
which are only and solely to be had by worshipping
the Father in spirit and truth; which is then only done
when your whole heart, and soul, and spirit trusts
wholly and solely **to the operation of that God
within you**, in whom we live, move, and have our
being. And be assured of this, as a most certain
truth, that we have neither more nor less of **the Divine
operation within us**, because of this or that outward
form or manner of our life, but just and strictly in that
degree, as our faith, and hope, and trust, and dependence upon God is more or less in us.

- - --------- -

In this passage there is an expression that must
be carefully weighed. It occurs twice. "When
your whole heart trusts wholly and solely *to the
operation of that God within you*, in whom we
live." "We have more or less of the *Divine operation within us*, just in that degree as our trust and
dependence upon God is more or less in us." It

is one of Law's favourite expressions in all his later writings. His last book, "An Humble Address to the Clergy,"[1] expounds, and proves, and applies with wonderful power the truth that all our religious goodness is to be had as wholly and solely from God's immediate operation, as we had our first goodness from Him at creation. That that which comforts, and enlightens, and blesses, which gives peace, and joy, and goodness, can be had in no other way but from God's immediate operation in us. He proves that the whole work of redemption in the soul of man is, and can be nothing else, but the inward, immediate, continual operation of Father, Son, and Holy Spirit, raising up again in the soul that first life to which our first father died.

Every believer accepts the truth of the operation of God within him, and believes that without it he cannot have the Divine life. But this general belief profits little, unless we not only understand, but with our whole heart believe, that this immediate continual operation of God is not one thing along with others through which we are blest, but the one essential thing to which alone we owe anything that is to be called religion or goodness.[2]

[1] "The Power of the Spirit. An Humble Address to the Clergy." By William Law. J. Nisbet & Co.
[2] In the "Spirit of Prayer" Law writes: "That thou mayest be more firmly assured that the resignation to and dependence upon the working of God's Spirit within thee is right and sound, I shall lay before thee two great, and fundamental, and infallible truths, which will be as a rock for thy faith to stand on. First, that through all the whole nature of things, *nothing* can do or be a real good to thy soul, but the operation of God upon it. Secondly, that all the dispensations of God from the fall of Adam, were only for this one end, to fit, prepare, and dispose the soul for the operation of the Spirit of God upon it. These two truths, well and deeply apprehended, put the soul in its

It is as this is apprehended that the need will be felt
of what is said in one passage—"your whole heart trusting solely and wholly to the operation of God within
you." The reasonableness and necessity will be seen
of the demand that our whole life should become nothing but a meek, humble, patient resignation to God
and His power. And our whole soul will be filled with
abhorrence of that self which usurps God's place, pro-
fesses to do God's work, and robs us of our heavenly
birthright : God Himself living and working in us.

Let every one who would be a true Christian ponder
deeply the fact that more than he can conceive depends
upon his becoming intimately acquainted with this
operation of the Triune God within him; and what
is still more, upon his continually experiencing it.

24. Our Heart the Way to God.

Theophilus.—What a folly, then, to be so often
perplexed about the way to God ! For **nothing is the
way to God but our heart**; God is nowhere else to be
found, and the heart itself cannot find Him, or be
helped by anything else to find Him, but by its own
love of Him, faith in Him, dependence upon Him,
resignation to Him, and expectation of all from Him.

These are short, but full, articles of true religion,
which carry salvation along with them, which make a
true and full offering and oblation of our whole nature
to the Divine operation, and also a true and full confession of the Holy Trinity in unity. For, as they look

right state, in a continual dependence upon God, in a readiness
to receive all good from Him. All that is Grace, Redemption,
Salvation, is nothing else but so much of the life and operation
of God found again in the soul."

F

wholly to the Father, as blessing us with the operation of His own Word and Spirit, so they truly confess and worship the Holy Trinity of God. And as
they ascribe all to, and expect all from, this Deity
alone, so they make the truest and best of all con-
fessions, that there is no God but one.

Your foundation standeth sure whilst you look for
all your salvation through the Father, working life in
your soul by His own Word and Spirit, which dwell
in Him, and are one life both in Him and you.

"Nothing is the way to God but our heart." This is
a hard saying. You thought your heart was your
great hindrance on the way to God. The state of your
heart is your continual sorrow, and almost leads you to
despair. How can it be that the heart is the way to
God? And yet it is so. Your heart is your life; and
your life can only be altered by that which is the real
working of your heart. You can know nothing of God,
can receive no grace, can experience no working of the
Divine presence or power, but in the heart. The heart
cannot find God but by its own faith in Him, and
expectation of all from Him. All our salvation is in the
heart. Scripture speaks very awful things of the natural,
evil heart, and it says very wonderful and blessed
things of the regenerate heart. It is when the penitent
sinner listens to Scripture that he learns to know, what
he never thought or saw, how evil his heart is. If the
believer would listen to and believe what Scripture says
of the new heart His Father hath given him, with the
Holy Spirit sent into it to dwell in it and to keep it, and
fit it for everything it has to do, he would understand

and rejoice in the word: our heart the way to God, because there and there alone, but there most surely, the effectual operation of the Holy Trinity is carried on.

You say you feel or observe so little of this operation within you. I can well believe it. The reason is because it is a Divine, hidden working, to be accepted in faith before it is felt. And because the most Christians do not take time and stillness and trouble in God's presence to give themselves wholly to this working, and to get the spiritual assurance of its being carried on effectually, they cannot know it. As we had it in the last sentence of the previous paragraph, we have more or less of the Divine operation within us, just and strictly in that degree as our faith, and trust, and dependence upon God is more or less in us. No wonder, when we take so little trouble to live by the faith of this operation of God, that we know so little of it.

And how is this to be remedied? By ceasing to look at what we can see in our hearts, and concentrating our whole strength upon believing what God is doing there, and waiting to do. Science tells us that however strong the wind is that sweeps the surface of the sea, and however high the waves may run, in the unseen depths below all is perfect calm and rest. It is even so with the new heart. On the surface the winds that blow may raise storms, and in the multitude of our thoughts and doubts, our resolutions and prayers, our efforts and failures, all may be perplexity and darkness. But lower down there is a hidden depth where the Spirit of God dwells and the peace of God reigns. But you do not know it, and have no benefit from it, because you never have let the sounding line of faith down to where the Spirit hides Himself from sight. He refuses to discover Himself to anything but a childlike, trustful faith. Oh, begin and honour the Holy Spirit and Triune God, as they dwell and work in you, by never thinking of your heart without believing and rejoicing that God is there. God has given you the new heart, cleansed by faith, with the love of God shed abroad by the indwelling Spirit, amid the surrounding sin that dwells in your flesh. That sin is ever seeking to enter; it does enter and get the upper hand the moment you cease believing and yielding to the Divine operation. As often as the motions of sin arise, lose no time in seeking either to condemn or to conquer them, but retire at once into your fortress, the secret place of the Most High, by believing that God through His Spirit is in you. He will mortify the deeds of the body and of the heart, which have been such a weariness to you. You will say, "My heart rejoiceth." I beseech you, as earnestly as you believe in the mighty power of God working in you, believe that your heart is its scene, is His abode and working-place. Let your heart be very sacred, as the palace and temple of the King! You will then say with joy: "Our heart the way to God."

Now read the passage over again, and say if you do not begin to see better why a meek, humble, patient resignation to God, as a state of heart, is the one condition of really, truly finding and appropriating Christ, is the one only way of dying to self, is the one only way to God Himself, and the experience of His presence and power in the soul.

FOURTH SECTION.

OF THE LIFE OF GOD IN THE SOUL.

25. *The Lamb of God Breathing His Nature into us.*

Theogenes.—I can never enough thank you, Theophilus, for this good and comfortable answer to my scrupulous fear. It seems now as if I could always know how to find full relief in this humble, meek, patient, total resignation of myself to God. It is, as you said, a remedy that is always at hand, equally practicable at all times, and never in greater reality than when my own tempers are making war against it in my own heart.

You have quite carried your point with me; the God of patience, meekness, and love is the one God of my heart. It is now the whole bent and desire of my soul to seek for all my salvation in and through the merits and mediation of the meek, humble, patient, resigned, suffering Lamb of God, who alone hath power to bring forth the blessed birth of these heavenly virtues in my soul. He is the bread of God that came down from heaven, of which the soul must eat, or perish and pine in everlasting hunger. He is the eternal love and meekness, that left the bosom of His Father, to be Himself the resurrection of meekness and love in all the darkened, wrathful

souls of fallen men. What a comfort is it to think
that this Lamb of God, Son of the Father, Light of the
world, who is the glory of heaven and the joy of
angels, is as near to us, as truly in the midst of us,
as He is in the midst of heaven ! And that not a
thought, look, and desire of our heart that presses
towards Him, longing to catch, as it were, one small
spark of His heavenly nature, but is in as sure a way
of finding Him, touching Him, and drawing virtue
from Him, as the woman who was healed by longing
to touch the border of His garment.

In some previous passages we saw how closely Christ
and the virtues which accompany the death to self are
connected. We saw that the desire after these virtues
is a desire after Him in whom alone they are found, is a
turning to Him with the desire of being led and governed
by His Spirit of meekness, humility, and resignation to
God. We are now led a step farther. Theogenes sees
that God is the God of patience, meekness, and love,
and says, " It is now the whole bent and desire of my
heart to seek for all my salvation through the merits and
mediation of the meek, humble, patient, resigned, suffering Lamb of God, *who alone hath power to bring forth
the blessed birth of these virtues* in my soul." All the
teaching about turning to these virtues, and so dying to
self, was only to show the soul what was needed to
waken desire, and so prepare for a living, true faith in
the Lamb of God and what He has to impart to us.

Christ not only died for sin as a guilt, but to sin as a
power. It came to Him with its temptation, its promises, and its threats. He resisted unto blood. In its

rage it slew Him. He died to it and all its power. He was for ever beyond its reach. Just as Adam—and in him we—died to God and heaven when he rejected them, so in Christ and with Christ we died to sin and its power. It is only as, by a faith wrought by the Holy Spirit, we accept God's declaration that we are dead to sin in Christ, and reckon ourselves to be so, that we are able to take up the true position towards sin, as those who know they are delivered from its power. In this lies hid the secret of true holiness.

And what, now, was the disposition that animated Christ in His death, the spirit that gave it its worth and power and made it a death of sin? It was the humility that bowed under the curse of sin, the meekness that bore all God and man laid on Him, the patience that let God take His own time, the resignation in perfect obedience to His will and love. Through this alone it was that He died to sin and rose to live to God. And it is through this spirit alone that the death to sin in Christ enters and masters the believer's life. At creation man was made to live in humble dependence on God. In the fall this was the one thing that he lost—his self-assertion ruined him. In redemption this was the one thing he needed, to be brought back to his blessed place of humility and resignation to God. In Christ this was the one thing by which and for which He saved us, as the meek and lowly Lamb of God. He wrought out for us, and by His own Spirit made us partakers of, a human nature of which humility was the chief glory.

And every believer who is seeking to apprehend Christ in the power of His death to sin, or has apprehended it, and longs to know its power, has ever, before everything else, in all His intercourse with God, just to sink down in humility and meekness before God. That is his proof that he shares in the death of Christ; that is his surrender of self to death ever anew. It is that will keep him from trusting not a false or imaginary Christ, but the very Lamb of God whose humility opened for Him and for us the way to the glory of God.

Do you see it? This humility, meekness, and surrender to God in which the death to self consists, is to be found in Christ alone. Seek them with your whole heart. Seek them in Him by a spirit-breathed faith that makes you one with Him, and receive from Him, the Lamb of God, these virtues in which His salvation consists, which He waits to bring forth in you. Read now again the last paragraph of our passage.

26. *The Marks of the Beast.*

Theogenes.—This doctrine also makes me quite weary and ashamed of all my own natural tempers, as so many marks of the beast upon me; every whisper of my soul that stirs up impatience, uneasiness, resentment, pride, and wrath within me shall be rejected with a "Get thee behind me, Satan;" for it is his, and has its whole nature from him. To rejoice in a resentment gratified appears now to me to be quite frightful. For what is it in reality but rejoicing that my own serpent of self has new life and strength given to it, and that the precious Lamb of God is denied entrance into my soul. For this is the strict truth of the matter. For to give in to resentment, and go willingly to gratify it, is calling up the courage of your own serpent, and truly helping it to be more stout and valiant and successful in you. On the other hand, to give up all resentment of every kind, and on every occasion, however artfully, beautifully, outwardly coloured, and **to sink down into the humility of meekness** under all contrariety, contradiction, and injustice, always turning the other cheek to the smiter, however haughty, is the best of all prayers, the surest of all means, to have nothing but Christ living and working in you, as the Lamb of God, that taketh away every sin that ever had power over your soul.

What a blindness was it in me to think that I had no covetousness because the love of pelf was not felt by me? For to covet is to desire; and what can it signify whether I desire this or that? If I desire anything but that which God would have me to be and do, I stick in the mire of covetousness, and must have all that evil and disquiet living and working in me which robs misers of their peace both with God and man.

Once again we are led to think of self and its works. Theogenes confesses how he now begins to see what the evil is of giving way to resentment, and what the folly of thinking that covetousness only meant a miser's love of money.

Of the former he says that he now sees that his natural tempers are all so many marks of the beast. That to give in to resentment residing in the heart is nothing but rejoicing; that the serpent of self has new life and strength given to it, is calling up the courage of your own serpent, and helping it to be more successful in you. He sees that to sink down into the humility of meekness under all contradictions and injustice is the surest means to have Christ living in you as the Lamb of God who taketh away every sin that ever had power over a soul.

There are two lessons we have to learn here. The one is, that when we speak of the death to self, we must beware of not confining it to our relation to God, and using strong language about our nothingness before Him, while in our intercourse with our fellow-men self seeks and has its own way. The humility and meekness and patience and resignation to God which we seek, which we see in the Lamb of God, for which we turn to Him in faith, are specially needed for, and must be proved in our intercourse with men. It may be easy to try and humble ourselves before the great God—who would not do that?—but before our fellow-sinners—it is this that is hard. It is this the Lamb of God can give. His meekness stood the test of man's provocation and ingratitude. If ours is to do so, we need every morning, every hour, to sink down into Christ's humility, and believe in it as our only safeguard in daily life, our only strength to walk in lowliness and love all the day.

The other lesson is, that every rising or outbreak of evil, of anger, or selfishness, or pride must ever be regarded as a mark of the beast—a proof of the presence of the serpent in our paradise, and at once urge us to turn to the Lamb of God, not only for deliverance from that outbreak, but for that promised indwelling by which the Spirit of Love becomes our whole life, and we are made more than conquerors through Him who loved us, and in His love makes His abode with us. It is the promised seed alone, in His indwelling presence, can bruise the serpent's head.

All this is equally true of what Theogenes says of his great mistake about covetousness being only love of money. "If I desire anything but that which God would have me be or do, I stick in the mire of covetousness." If we look at the extent to which Christians indulge with the world, in the pursuit of comforts and luxuries, of pleasures and possessions—if we think of what a large part of the attention and devotion of the soul is given to being, and having, and doing all we see others around us are, and have, and do, we cannot wonder that the self which is fostered and nourished by all this should in other directions exercise an irresistible power.

Everything points us to the one thing. It avails little to resist the workings of self; a death to self is our only hope. We must die to self; and that death the Lamb of God died for us that He might share it with us. As we gaze upon the cross in the humility, and meekness, and patience, and resignation to God He showed there, let us turn to Him, with the desire to be like Him, with the faith that makes us like Him. Let us in His name sink down in deep humility and meekness, and give and leave ourselves in God's hands.

27. *Oh, Sweet Resignation to God!*

Theogenes.—Oh, sweet resignation of myself to God, happy death of every selfish desire, blessed unction of a holy life, the only driver of all evil out of my soul! be thou my guide and governor wherever I go! Nothing but thee can take me from myself, nothing but thee can lead me to God; hell has no power where thou art, nor can heaven hide itself from thee. Oh, may I never indulge a thought, bring forth a word, or do anything for myself or others, but under the influence of this blessed inspiration.

Forgive, dear Theophilus, this transport of my soul! I could not stop it. The sight, though distant, of this Heavenly Canaan, this Sabbath of the soul, freed from the miserable labour of self, **to rest in meekness, humility, patience, and resignation under the Spirit of God,** is like the joyful voice of the Bridegroom to my soul, and leaves no wish in me but to be at the marriage-feast of the Lamb.

Oh, sweet resignation of myself to God! Happy death of every selfish desire! Blessed unction of a holy life! All the teaching of the previous pages is gathered up in this passage. Resignation to God includes everything that has been said on the humility, meekness, and patience of the Lamb of God. It reminds us, what we cannot repeat too often or study too earnestly, that man was created to receive all his goodness and happiness from God in an unceasing direct communication; and that therefore the giving up himself to God is the root of all religion and blessedness. Christ came to restore us to that state: there was no possibility of anything better or higher—to live in unceasing blessed dependence on God. He came to live out a human life, as Adam should have lived it, with the meekness and lowliness of a lamb as its spirit. He so conquered sin and redeemed us from its power, that He can live this life in us, and make resignation into God's hands the habitual spirit of our life. It was His humbling Himself fitted Him to be our Saviour; it is His humility is our salvation. Salvation is making us humble as He was.

It often takes a long time before this truth, even when known and accepted, fully dawns on the soul. We then begin to see: As there is only one God, so, for the creature and the sinner, the one duty towards Him is the humility that gives Him His place, and is content to receive everything from Him alone. We begin to see that in every prayer, in every thought, in every moment of our life, we need just one thing—to take the place of humility and dependence before God, of a meek and patient resignation or giving up of ourselves into God's hands. This humility will then no longer be to us one among a number of other virtues, not even the chief of all the virtues, but the one essential condition and root of the life of grace. We shall see that all other graces —peace, love, joy, faith, devotion, service—have their beginning here, because it alone places and keeps us in the posture of dependence, where God can work in us.

Oh, sweet resignation to God! It is hardly necessary to remind the reader that the word has not only a passive sense, as we apply it to a meek and patient submission to His will in providence, but also includes the exercise of the active power of obedience, as the surrender to the performance of His commands. In prophecy God had revealed the work Christ had to do as well as the sufferings He had to endure; both were equally to Him the will of God; He gave Himself with a perfect resignation into the will of God to do all He commanded and to suffer all He appointed. We may often find that as we long to turn to Christ in true humility, meekness, and patience, under a sense of our impotence and nothingness, there is still something that hinders and disturbs our finding perfect rest. See whether it be not this, that in something or other, in some little thing perhaps, we are still doing our own will, or are not careful to know fully all that God wills. Full resignation to God's will, a whole-hearted giving up of ourselves to the blessed perfect will of God, will bring perfect rest. Let the resignation of submission ever be accompanied by the resignation of obedience.

"Oh, sweet resignation of myself to God! be thou

my guide and governor wherever I go! Nothing but thee can take me from myself; nothing but thee can lead me to God! Freed from the miserable labour of self, to rest in meekness, humility, patience, and resignation under the Spirit of God, is like the joyful voice of the Bridegroom to my soul." Let every one who is seeking for the birth of the Spirit of Love in his soul, and is willing to sell all that he may become the owner of the treasure, of which even the sight is so delightful, listen again to and mark well the voice of his guide: "Humble yourselves under the mighty hand of God; He shall exalt you in due time." Bow and rest under the covering of the Spirit in the humility, meekness, patience, and resignation of the Lamb of God. Make it your one care, your one desire, your continual prayer and practice, to learn of Him who is meek and lowly of heart: ye shall find rest to your soul. Seek only the one thing—to come out of self in giving up all to God, to walk before God in the fellowship of Christ's death to sin and self, to keep the very lowest place before God, and He in His love and power will in due time exalt you.

28. *The Marriage Feast of the Lamb.*

Theophilus.—Thither, Theogenes, you must certainly come, if you keep to the path of meekness, humility, and patience, under a full resignation to God. But if you go aside from it, let the occasion seem ever so glorious, or the effects ever so wonderful to you, it is only preparing for yourself a harder death. For die you must, to all and everything that you have worked or done under any other spirit but that of meekness, humility, and true resignation to God.

Everything else, be it what it will, hath its rise from the fire of nature; it belongs to nothing else, and must of all necessity be given up, lost, and taken from you again by fire, either here or hereafter.

For these virtues are the only wedding garments; they are the lamps and vessels well furnished with oil.

There is nothing that will do in the stead of them; they must have their own full and perfect work in you, or the soul can never be delivered from its fallen, wrathful state. And all this is no more than is implied in this Scripture doctrine, viz., that there is no possibility of salvation but in and by the birth of the meek, humble, patient, resigned Lamb of God in our souls. And when this Lamb of God has brought forth a real birth of His own meekness, humility, and full resignation to God in our souls, then are our lamps trimmed and our virgin hearts made ready for the marriage feast.

This marriage feast signifies the entrance into the highest state of union that can be between God and the soul in this life.

―――――――

Keep to the path of meekness, humility, and patience, under a full resignation to God. These virtues are the only wedding garments: they are the lamps and vessels well furnished with oil. There is nothing will do instead of them. All this is implied in the Scripture doctrine, that there is no possibility of salvation but in and by the birth of the meek, humble, patient, resigned Lamb of God in our soul.

In a previous passage we read of the meek and patient Lamb of God, who alone hath power to bring forth the birth of these heavenly virtues in the soul. Here we come one step still farther ; our salvation is by the birth of the meek, humble, patient, resigned Lamb of God Himself in our souls. It is when this Lamb of God, by giving Himself within us, has brought forth a real birth of His own meekness, patience, and full resignation to God in our souls, that our virgin hearts are made ready for the marriage feast—the highest state of union between God and the soul that can be in this life. This was the union between God and the soul for which man was created here on earth, in a life of loving, adoring humility and dependence, receiving all from God even as Christ when on earth. This is redemption and this is salvation, when Christ as the Lamb of God is formed in and dwells within us, and in the love that passeth knowledge fills us with the fulness of God.

To all this, humility and resignation to God is the only entrance and the sure access. It alone is deliverance from self: it follows the Lamb whithersoever He goeth ; it yields the whole being to, and receives the full operation of the power of God in the heart. It is itself the highest blessedness, freedom from all desire that is not after God, the very image of God's Son, the object of His complacency and delight, the only adornment He seeks in the temple in which He dwells.

Blessed Humility! how shall we seek and find thee? Turn the whole desire of thy heart towards it, seeking soul. Sink down into thy own nothingness. Lift up thine eyes to the God of glory looking on thee and loving thee, and waiting to give and work all in thee. And if thou findest there is that in thee which will not, which cannot be humble, turn thy longing eyes to the Lamb of God. *There is the humility of God prepared for thee.* There thou hast thy Redeemer, who gives thee all He is and has. Let this be thy humility, that thou dost confess thou hast none of thy own, that thou art content to receive His as thine, and so to abide in thy nothingness, while all the glory is His. Let every desire for humility draw thee out of thyself to the meekness and gentleness of Christ. Then, with every thought of Christ, turn into thy heart with the assured faith that this is thy salvation, the birth of the meek, humble Lamb of God in thy soul.

And if the fear comes that all thy longing for Him and turning to Him and believing in Him is too feeble, just remember, it is His own Holy Spirit, who has wakened these desires and this love of humility, who is moving and drawing thee towards Himself. He who has worked in thee the beginnings of a love of humility, will, with Divine certainty and power, beget within thee the meekness and resignation of the Holy Lamb of God.

29. *The Birthday of the Spirit of Love.*

Theophilus.—This marriage feast signifies the entrance into the highest state of union that can be between God and the soul in this life; or, in other words, it is **the birthday of the Spirit of Love** in our souls, which, whenever we attain, will feast our souls with such peace and joy in God as will blot out the remembrance of everything that we called peace or joy before.

All that we have said to-day of the necessity of the fallen soul's dying to self, **by meekness, patience, humility, and full resignation to God,** is strictly the same thing, and asserted from the same ground, as when it was said that the three first properties

G

of nature must have their wrathful activity taken from
them by the light of God breaking in upon them, or
manifesting itself in them.

Therefore, as sure as the light of God, or the
entrance of the Deity into the three first properties
of nature, is absolutely necessary to make nature to
be a heavenly kingdom of light and love, so sure and
certain is it that the creaturely life, that is fallen from
God under the wrathful first properties of nature, can
have no deliverance from it, cannot have a birth of
heavenly light and love, by any other possible way
but that of dying, to self, by meekness, humility,
patience, and full resignation to God.

And the reason is this. It is because the will is
the leader of the creaturely life, and it can have
nothing but that to which its will is turned. And
therefore it cannot be saved from, or raised out of,
the wrath of nature, till its will turns from nature,
and wills to be no longer driven by it. But it cannot
turn from nature, or show a will to come from under
its power, any other way than by turning and giving
up itself to that meekness, humility, patience, and
resignation to God, which, so far as it goes, is a
leaving, rejecting, and dying to all the guidance of
nature.

And thus you see that this one simple way is,
according to the immutable nature of things, the one
only possible and absolutely necessary way to God.
It is as possible to go two contrary ways at once, as
to go to God any other way than this.

We are now coming to the close of Law's book on
the Spirit of Love, and to the special point this third
Dialogue was to deal with. He had started with the one
truth that God is Love—an infinite and unchangeable
will to communicate all His own goodness and blessedness to His creatures, and that this love of God was
meant to be our life. After expounding how creation
and redemption were the manifestation of this love, he
had undertaken, in this Golden Dialogue, to teach the
way for us to enter into it, and really be blessed with
the Spirit of Love filling our hearts. Having shown
us the need of an actual Divine birth of this love
within us, the deadly evil of self, and the necessity of
dying to it, if this new life is to be born in us, he opened
up the one only way to this death—that living faith
in the Lamb of God which receives Him into the heart,
with those virtues which constituted Him a Saviour, a
meek and humble resignation and obedience to God.
When this Lamb of God has brought forth a real birth
of His own meekness, humility, and resignation to God
in our souls, then are (our virgin hearts) made ready for
the marriage feast—*then is the birthday of the Spirit of
Love in our souls.*

This is surely nothing more or less than our Blessed
Lord meant when He spoke of our abiding in His love,
even as He abode in the Father's love. And he makes
it such a blessed possibility, such a Divine certainty, by
telling us that as the Father loved Him, even so has He
loved us. It was the Father's love to Him, when He
slept an unconscious infant on His mother's knee, or
hung on the cross, or lay in the grave—it was the Infinite
Love of God that kept Him, and filled His heart. That
love was His life. It is with that same love Christ loves
us now. If we only believe in its infinite lovingness and
longing to impart itself to us and get possession of us—

for that is the very nature of love, and the very power Divine love has—how we should count upon the love holding us fast, and open our whole hearts to be filled with it. To the soul that in utter self-despair will die to self, and meekly yield itself to God to do His work, there is a birthday of the Spirit of Love, and entrance into Christ's love to abide there, and have it abide in him.

And the way to abide there, when we have entered, is so simple and so sure. Jesus says, "If ye keep My commandments, ye shall abide in My love ; even as I kept My Father's commandments and abide in His love." Some think the abiding in the love an impossibility, because the keeping of the commands is impossible. Our Lord surely does not mock us by telling of a way that cannot bring us to the blessed life He offers. No, He assures us that we are to keep the commandments, *even as He kept them.* God is our Husbandman, who cares for the branches as much as for the Vine, and works in them all He worked in Him. Christ is our Vine, to impart all His life and spirit and strength to us, His branches. Christ the Loving One is Christ the obedient One : He imparts His obedience as much as His love. His love enables us to obey. Oh, do not think that Christ speaks of abiding in His love as an impossble blessing, or keeping His commandments as an impiossible way. Would you mock a hungry cripple at your door by inviting him in to an abundant meal that was waiting, when you knew he could not rise to come in? Would you not help him in? And can we not count upon our Lord Jesus, when He flung the door wide open—"Abide in My love "—and when He points out the way in which He walked, which He Himself is—" Keep My commandments "—to bring us in? Do let us turn in meekness and humility to the meek and lowly Lamb of God; He will bring forth in our souls His own humility and that obedient resignation to God which can and will keep the commands.

"Love is the Christ of God; wherever it comes, it comes as the blessing and happiness of every natural life, as the restorer of every lost perfection, a redeemer from all evil, a fulfiller of all righteousness, and a peace of God which passeth all understanding. Through all the universe of things, nothing is unsatisfied or restless, but because its nature has not attained the full birth of the Spirit of Love." "Abide in My love:" the infinite love of Jesus stretches out its arms, and longs to take us up in its embrace, longs to have our heart for its abode. Let our religion become more a faith in, and intercourse with, and obedience to, a personal Lord Jesus, loving us personally and tenderly; we shall soon believe and know and feel that there is such a blessing as the birthday of the Spirit of Love. And if we have not yet attained, let us turn in great simplicity and humility to the Lamb of God, who alone can bring forth this birth in them that follow Him whithersoever He goeth.

30. *This Way to God Absolutely Infallible.*

Theophilus.—But what is best of all, this way absolutely infallible; nothing can defeat it. And all this infallibility is fully grounded in the twofold character of our Saviour—(1) As He is the Lamb of God, a principle and source of all meekness and humility in the soul. And (2) as He is the Light of eternity, that blesses eternal nature, and turns it into a kingdom of heaven.

For, in this twofold respect, He has a power of redeeming us, which nothing can hinder; but, sooner or later, He must see all His and our enemies under His feet, and all that is fallen in Adam into death must rise and return into a unity of an eternal life in God.

For as the Lamb of God He has all power to bring forth in us a sensibility and a weariness of our own wrathful state, and a willingness to fall from it into meekness, humility, patience, and resignation to that mercy of God which alone can help us. And when we are thus weary and heavy laden, and willing to get rest to our souls in meek, humble, patient resignation to God, then it is that He, as the light of God and heaven, joyfully breaks in upon us, turns our darkness into light, our sorrow into joy, and begins that kingdom of God and Divine love within us which will never have an end.

In a passage of exquisite beauty and depth, the whole teaching of the book is now summed up. The reason is given why this one simple way of turning to the Lamb of God is the only and infallible way. The reason is this: because the two sides of the truth that have been presented, dying to self and living in love, are found perfectly united in Christ as the Lamb of God.

As the Lamb, He is on the one hand the principle and source of all meekness and humility in the soul. On earth He humbled Himself to enter into our weakness, and both in life and death He proved Himself the meek and patient Lamb of God. He was and did all this for no other reason but that He might work out such a nature and disposition as we needed, and impart it to us. In carrying out this, His blessed saving work, it is He who wakens in us the sense of weariness with our own sin, and makes us willing to sink down under it into the meekness, humility, patience, and resignation to that mercy of God which alone can help us.

We need to believe this. The work of the Lamb of God is not only to die and atone for our sin. By no means. But it is to be our leader in that path of submission and obedience in which alone the creature can be blessed. As Leader, He really leads us, drawing us on, inspiring and enabling us to walk in His footsteps. If we now would only believe that every feeling of weariness and unrest, every sense of evil and impotence, is the stirring of His Spirit within us, how we should turn from all our struggles and self-reproach, in stillness to yield to His working, and in meek and humble resignation to expect deliverance nowhere but from God Himself.

When the soul has thus known and bowed before Him, then, as the Lamb on the throne in that city of God, of which it is said, "The Lamb is the Light thereof," He rises upon the soul as the Light of Heaven, and begins that Divine kingdom of love within us which shall never have an end. The Lamb of God, meek and lowly of heart, can give rest to our souls in no other way but by making us partakers of His meekness and lowliness. Do let us believe that, as we accept that meekness and lowliness on earth as our dwelling-place, as the air we breathe, and the light in which we walk, the Lamb on the throne will make Himself known to us in His heavenly life and power, and shine into us with the light of the glory of God. The meekness and lowliness of earth are inseparably linked to the light and the love of heaven. Bow in all thy sinfulness and feebleness in meek and patient resignation to God, and rest there; thou mayest be assured the Light of God will rise on thee.

The death to sin, and to self as its instrument, in the fellowship with Christ, the Lamb of God, gives an infallible entrance, even in this life, into a life in the light and love of God.

Seek fellowship with Him in His meekness on earth; receive Him in His lowliness into your heart as its one hope and love, and you may be sure His glory, as the Lamb on the throne, will become your light. Give Him a place in the depth of your heart, and, with every rising of self, sink down in His presence in humility, and meekness, and stillness of soul. You will know Him as the Lamb on the throne.

31. *Salvation the Life of God in the Soul.*

Theophilus.—Need I say any more, Theogenes, to show you how to come out of the wrath of your evil earthly nature, into **the sweet peace and joy of the spirit of love?** Neither notions, nor speculations, nor heat, nor fervour, nor rules, nor methods, can bring it forth. It is the child of light, and cannot possibly have any birth in you but only and solely from the light of God rising in your own soul, as it rises in heavenly beings. But the light of God cannot arise or be found in you by any art or contrivance of your own, but only **and solely in the way of that meekness, humility, and patience, which waits, trusts, resigns to, and expects all from the inward, living, life-giving operation of the triune God within you;** creating, quickening, and reviving in your fallen soul that birth, and image, and likeness of the Holy Trinity, in which the first father of mankind was created.

Theogenes.—You need say no more, Theophilus; you have not only removed that difficulty which brought us hither, but have by a variety of things fixed and confirmed us in a full belief of that great truth elsewhere asserted, namely, "That there is but one salvation for all mankind, and that is the life of God in the soul. God is one, human nature is one, salvation is one, and the way to it is one, and that is the desire of the soul turned to God."

Therefore, dear Theophilus, adieu. If we see you no more in this life, you have sufficiently taught us how to seek and find every kind of goodness, blessing, and happiness in God alone.

Here we now have Law's summing up of the whole. He has shown us how to come out of the wrath and wretchedness of our evil, earthly nature into the sweet peace and joy of the Spirit of Love. But ere he parts he must first once again utter a word of warning. "Neither notions nor speculations, heat nor fervour, rules nor methods, can bring it forth." No clear reasonings nor beautiful mental conceptions of the truth, no warm feelings of admiration or earnest purpose to attain it, no strict obedience of laws of life or conduct can give it us: the Spirit of Love is the child of light, and cannot have any birth but from the light of God, in His own free grace and power rising on the soul. No art or contrivance of religion can bring it; it can arise only in that way of meekness, humility, and patience which expects all from the inward operation of the Triune God within you, creating again in your fallen soul the image of the Holy Trinity, that is, that likeness to God in his life and being in which our first father was created.

Can words make it plainer that our salvation is from God alone? And that our only hope of salvation is in turning to that Lamb of God who opened up the way to the Father, and now lives to lead us to the Father in the way of His own footsteps? And that all hindrance in the way of salvation, comes wholly and solely from the ignorance or the self-will that will not turn from its own efforts to the humility and meekness and patience and resignation to God, which the holy Lamb of God begets in them that trust in Him, and in which He causes the light of heaven to shine in the soul?

Let the warning with which Theophilus closes his teaching remind us of that with which he began. It is only by a birth from above, it is only by a birth from the Holy Spirit, that the Spirit of Love, that the love of God can enter and possess us. Let every lesson of this book, or of any book, or of God's Book, make us turn to the Holy Spirit, who is secretly dwelling and working in us to lead us in the true and living way, and to work in us what is needed, that the death to self and the life unto God may be our experience. *Of all that we see in the word, or in Christ, the Holy Spirit bears to us the truth and reality. What is above sense and reason He can work in the inward part.* With all we know or do not know, with all we feel or do not feel, with all we seek and have not yet found, let us turn meekly and humbly to the hidden operation of God's Spirit within us; through Him the Triune God will show forth in us all the riches of His glory, and lead us into His life of perfect love.

And let the parting words of Theogenes be ours : " You

have confirmed us in a belief of that great truth, that there is but one salvation, and that is the life of God in the soul. And that there is but one way to it, the desire of the soul turned to God. Therefore, dear Theophilus, adieu. You have sufficiently taught us how to seek and find every kind of goodness, blessing, and happiness in God alone."

NOTE A.

There is just one point on which a word of explanation may be needful—the expression Dying to Self. It is said that to speak of our dying to sin or self is at variance with Scripture, which teaches us that we *have died*, that we *are dead* to sin.

I am most deeply convinced of the importance of the blessed truth that we have died to sin in Christ, that our only strength for deliverance from its power is in the faith of Him, and that that faith is to manifest itself in our reckoning ourselves as dead unto sin and alive unto God in Christ Jesus our Lord. I am fully persuaded that only as, by the Holy Spirit, we accept this Divine revelation concerning ourselves, and live and act in it, we can experience that victory over sin which God has provided for us.

But how then still speak about dying to sin or self? My answer is this: The truth of the death to sin and self is so far beyond the spiritual capacity of most Christians, because the power of the Holy Spirit is so little known, that their hearts need to be prepared and their desires roused to seek after it. And I think that there is nothing that will so much help to this as Law's teaching in this little book. As he shows them what self is, why a death to self is the only way to be delivered from it, what the dispositions are which the death to self will be manifested in, how impossible it is for us to give ourselves these dispositions, how the sincere desire after them will lead us to the Lamb of God as the only One in whom and whose death they are to be found, and how faith in Him unites with Him in His death, the soul will be prepared to appreciate and accept the wondrous salvation of which Rom. vi. speaks. Dying to self is the duty of every sinner as the only way to be freed from that sinful self: as he somewhat understands this, and discovers his own utter impotence to effect it, the attempt to obey the command will prepare him for the glorious gospel, "Reckon yourselves dead." Dying to self is the expression of the willingness and endeavour that will alone prepare for the death to self provided in Christ.

This appears to be in harmony with the course our Lord took with His disciples when He commanded them to deny them-

Historical fact

Current happening

selves and take up their cross. Dying to self is nothing but entirely denying self. The one is as impossible as the other. And yet our Lord commanded it as the simple duty of those who would follow Him. How utterly the disciples failed we know. But the words helped to waken thought and desire, and so to prepare them for entering fully into the fellowship of *His* cross and *His* death.

There is still another point of view from which it appears very helpful. There are many who strive to reckon themselves dead in Christ, and yet know very little of what that death of our Lord, in which they share, meant to Him. They have never seen aright that the value of that death, and its power to atone for sin, consists entirely in the dispositions that animated Him in it. His humbling Himself as a servant, His obedience to the Father's will, His meekness and patience as the Lamb of God, His entire surrender of His will and His spirit into the Father's hands—it is in this Christ's death to sin consisted. Those who, reckoning themselves dead to sin, claim their partnership in Christ's death, need to know that it is not only a judicial, but an actual spiritual participation in all that His death means. To such there is nothing more needful or helpful than to have this indispensable need for dying to self unfolded to them. One great reason that our being dead to sin in Christ remains such an inexplicable mystery, or else such a powerless article of faith, is that they have never seen the need or the desirableness of a real dying to self. The teaching of dying to self may be the schoolmaster to Christ and the true death to self in Him. It is only as men see what they ought to be and do, and strive after it, and find they cannot attain to it, that the offer of a death in Christ will get meaning, and power, and attractiveness.

Those who are dead to sin and alive to God in Christ are called to yield themselves to God "as alive from the dead." Their whole life is to bear the death-marks, as Christ the Risen One bore the marks of the wounds. The most advanced believer will feel the need of ever studying more deeply the wonderful spirit of that death. Nothing will show more its perfect adaptation to our human life than ever to lay the two alongside each other, and in the study of our dying to self to learn what it is we are to find in our Lord's death to sin as it becomes ours. Our death and our living unto God unites us in Christ in a spiritual birth that must lead on to a spiritual growth, with the maintenance and development and application of all the powers contained in the birth as a bud. The two principles of death and life run together through the whole of the redeemed life. Paul thus says, "I die daily;" "Death worketh in me;" "Always bearing about the dying of Jesus." This death of Jesus to sin once for all completed on the cross, once for all given to the believer in regeneration, once for all seen and embraced when the Holy Spirit reveals it—this death to self has to be maintained as the law of our life in the daily denial of self. And this denial of self, surrender of self, this continual self-effacement in the power of our death to self in Christ, is nothing but the daily dying to self. The more complete our apprehension of the spiritual meaning of Christ's death to sin and ours in Him, the more whole-hearted will be our obedience to Christ's command to deny that self—the more real, in the power of His death working in us, our dying daily to it.

Once again: Christ's death for sin and to sin was not at the beginning but the end of His life. He needed to be prepared for it by a life in which he learned obedience. Souls that are not prepared by strong longing to be delivered from sin cannot apprehend this death to sin, or, if they think they do, they do not live it out. The school of denying self, humbling self, of dying to self with its failures and despair, is indispensable to entering into the full fellowship of death with Christ. Until a soul has been taught to give itself up to death, and found how vain it is, the free gift of a death to sin with Christ cannot be appreciated.

NOTE B.

There may be some who fear that all that is said of the birth of the Spirit of Love in us, of the setting up of the kingdom of God and of love in our heart, may lead souls to delight in their own perfection, and so to spiritual self-indulgence. Any one who remembers Law's definition of love will see how little his teaching would allow of this. Love in God is His unchangeable will to communicate all His own goodness to His creatures as far as they are capable of it. His love entering into us cannot change its nature: it still is a delight to impart itself to others and to bless them. It cannot help loving: it is rooted in the death of self, and leaves as little room for self-seeking towards man as towards God. It is the very spirit of God and of Christ towards men taking possession of us. It always leads to and gives power for devoted service for men.

The same result will be reached by looking at the Lamb of God in His humbling Himself to death. He did it only and solely for the sake of men. No one who truly seeks and enters into His humility, and meekness, and death but will there meet with that love which gave itself to save the perishing. True faith in the Lamb of God as the meek and lowly One must infallibly lead to a love unto death for men.

Whether we speak of the death to self or a sinking down in humility and meekness before God or faith in the Lamb of God, it all means one thing—a deliverance from self to find our liberty and our blessedness in the living sacrifice of ourselves for all around us.

THE END

Printed by BALLANTYNE, HANSON & Co.
Edinburgh & London

CPSIA information can be obtained at www.ICGtesting.com
Printed in the USA
BVOW03s1803230415

397239BV00010B/574/P